RALPH NADER
PRESENTS
A Citizens' Guide to Lobbying

RALPH NADER

☆ PRESENTS ☆

A Citizens' Guide to Lobbying

BY MARC CAPLAN

DEMBNER BOOKS   NEW YORK

About the Author

Marc Caplan was Director of the Connecticut Citizen Action Group from early 1974 to early 1980.

For the past three years, he has been Executive Director of the Legislative Electoral Action Program (LEAP), a broad coalition of citizens, labor, environmental, minority group, and women's organizations committed to electing progressive candidates to office in Connecticut.

He is a graduate of Duke University and Columbia University School of Law.

Dembner Books
Published by Red Dembner Enterprises Corp.
1841 Broadway, New York, N.Y. 10023
Distributed by W. W. Norton & Company, Inc.
500 Fifth Avenue, New York, N.Y. 10110

Library of Congress Cataloging in Publication Data
Caplan, Marc, 1946—
    Ralph Nader presents a citizens' guide to lobbying.

    Includes index.
    1. Lobbying—United States—Handbooks, manuals, etc.
1. Nader, Ralph.   II. Title.   III. Title: Citizens'
guide to lobbying.
JK1118.C25 1983   328.73'078'0202   83-2022
ISBN 0-934878-26-9
ISBN 0-934878-27-7 (pbk.)

Text design by Antler & Baldwin, Inc.

Contents

Preface

Suppose an individual knocked on your door and declared: "Hi, I'm your new neighbor down the street and I just wanted to let you know that I have the authority to increase your taxes, reduce your education budget, and imperil your health and safety. See you later!" You would be likely to call out: "Listen, come back here, I want to ask you some questions. You mean something to me."

Well, those "neighbors" are your state legislators. They make or repeal laws, check on the operations of state agencies, pass on state budgets, help decide the disposition of federal grants, and set the tone for either the integrity or corruption of state and local governments. They do, indeed, mean something to over two hundred million Americans. So it makes sense for you to mean something to them, besides receiving their flattery and being asked to vote for them at election time.

A democracy of active citizens recognizes that for elections to have substance and genuine choice, there needs to be a regular stream of citizen activity *between* elections. This effort can be viewed as a civic duty and/or as a civic hobby—your choice. Some active citizens I know see their work as important but still a burden. They do not usually stay at their dedication for very long. Others look at the civic calling as the essence of applied freedom, as a pleasure and more like a serious hobby than a chore. Hobbies invite skills as well as rewards; so does citizenship, and for very fundamental purposes—the constant shaping of a more just and happy society.

The process of learning and then actually advocating your positions before the legislature should be stimulating and fun. If you can be two-dimensional in this regard—being involved as well as being able to observe the tug and pull of legislating from a distance—you will achieve the craftsmanship and the perspective necessary to raise your work to the level of joy.

It helps to know that state legislatures are becoming more important by the year as more programs and responsibilities are being shifted to the states from the national government. At the same time, revenue-producing sources are not being shifted to the states by Washington. In addition, there is a growing trend of corporate lobbies moving for federal pre-emption of state authority, from banking to nuclear power regulation. This is occurring just at a time when the states are taking on more obligations to meet new or worsening problems. All these eddies and maelstroms of power can occur at the grievous expense of the communities if there is no regular vigilance and participation by informed citizens.

This volume grew out of the concentrated experience of a statewide group known as the Connecticut Citizen Action Group (CCAG). We helped start CCAG in 1971. Since that time, hundreds of people of diverse backgrounds and ages, who used to say "What's the use?" or "You can't fight City Hall" have become confident, goal-oriented citizen doers. But not without sometimes hesitating or making their last mistake their best teacher. A reservoir of experience about what works and what does not when approaching state legislatures began to build year after year. Marc Caplan and his associates at CCAG have distilled their experience in this book so you can share and build on it without having to reinvent many of the little wheels on the way to legislative success.

State legislatures are often nobody's business except businesses' business. Sound reporting about how these lawmakers behave under the influence of industrial and commercial lobbyists has made even caricature an understatement, especially near the end of a legislative session. If Congress was the best money could buy, to use the words of Oklahoma sage Will Rogers, 50 years ago, state legislatures have been, by and large, the worst money could buy or rent or wine and dine or bribe or employ. As one Maryland political observer once said: "The difference between Congress and state legislatures is that the latter do not attempt a pretense of probity nor an essay into statesmanship. Both attributes are not even treated as matters for style, much less for substance."

There are reasons for such differences. State legislatures often receive less media scrutiny, have much fewer full-time staff and other research resources, and possess little tradition of investigatory hearings. The lawmakers are more afflicted with direct conflicts of interest at the state level because they are mostly part-time. The rest of their time is devoted to other occupations such as selling real estate or insurance, or practicing law. More recently, special interests, largely corporatist, are perfecting the technology of lobbying—from mass mailings to their members to political action committees to a kind of job or environmental blackmail ("If you do not give us what we want, we'll have to close our plant or move to another state"). These pressures, particularly in difficult economic times, further the imbalances between the commercial lobbies and citizen groups. But this appraisal is not all-inclusively axiomatic by any means. Citizens have been flexing their muscles in consumer, environmental, tax reform, and open government areas with some success. The past fifteen years have witnessed a modest surge of ever more skilled efforts. Now it is time to dramatically up both the horsepower and the horizons.

Presently, the bulk of citizen advocacy at the state legislature relates to specific remedies or protections. These include economic rights and entitlements (stopping consumer fraud or maintaining social services, for example) or health and safety rights (combating pollution, hazardous nursing homes, or street crime). Keeping laws from being weakened by corporate power is also receiving more attention.

Future activities will continue to deal with these concerns, but must be expanded to cover empowerment issues that would facilitate the organization and exercise of citizen power. One model would make it much easier for consumers to band together in advocacy and bargaining associations with full-time staffs accountable to the members.

There are other parts of the empowerment agenda. They are the initiative, referendum, and recall, which over half of the states still do not recognize in their constitutions. There is the spread of consumer-owned cooperatives giving consumers group buying power and more political strength. There is the reform of electoral practices and campaign financing. And there is greater access to the electronic media by the audience.

Historically, our country has progressed in proportion to the shifts of power from the few to the many, starting with 1775, then the Constitution, and on through the populist-progressive periods to the assertion of rights by workers, minorities, women, and consumers in the past two generations. The rapid concentration of multinational corporate power over markets, media, and government is breeding new needs for an updated program shifting more instruments of power back to the citizenry. It is simply irresponsible to demand that people be more responsible and self-reliant while denying them crucial tools for responsible democratic action. This split between power and responsibility is manifest throughout our political economy, including the separation of property *ownership* (stocks, pension funds, savings deposits, public airwaves, and the public lands) from property *control* (in corporate hands) to the hollowness of voting rights for candidates who are placed on auction blocks.

If crises bring out the valor of a resourceful people, then

more people must now start doing more citizen work with the courage and creativity inherent in rising to major challenges. By investing just a small amount of time—a few hours a month or a few days a year—you and your friends and neighbors can mean something to your state legislators. The improvement that can result would be visible and sometimes astonishing.

A Citizens' Guide to Lobbying provides the reader, the avid aspirant for civic advances, with a careful and realistic trek into the land of state legislative advocacy. The materials flow logically and with ample illustrations. While the location is in Connecticut, the use of this know-how and strategy for affecting other state legislatures is quite convenient. All too frequently, full-time citizen activists remain so occupied with the struggles that they spare no hours to reflect, assemble, and communicate what they are learning. It is heartening to present to you the fruits of one citizen group's determination to take some time out and make this contribution to the expanding foundations of America's civic culture.

Ralph Nader
Washington, D.C.
June 1983

Acknowledgments

A Citizens' Guide to Lobbying is the product of several years of lobbying experience by the Connecticut Citizen Action Group, and was written by CCAG staff members. Much of the book was written by five lobbying novices who worked as CCAG advocates in the 1975 legislative session: Shirli Axelrod, Jerry Coursey, Bruce Dorpalen, Louise Garfield, and David Winkler. Veteran staff lobbyists Judy Blei, Julie Mannarino, Brian Sullivan, and John Wanchek added their insights. I coordinated the effort and added four chapters—The Press, Fundraising, After the Session, and the Conclusion. Special thanks for editorial assistance go to Bruce Ballenger, Joan Bethell, Ron Brownstein, Tim Massad, Marilyn Osterman, John Richard, and Andrew Stephens.

M. C.

Readers are encouraged to comment on the book. Please send your comments to:

John Richard
Citizen Action Group
P.O. Box 19312
Washington, D.C. 20036

Introduction

Over a drink at a Hartford watering hole, an insurance executive talks shop with his friend — an insurance broker who chairs the state legislature's insurance committee. The executive explains why legislation is needed to boost the industry's position. He hands over a bill drafted by his firm's stable of high-priced lawyers. After a few pleasantries, the two men shake hands and part.

They meet again a few weeks later at a poorly attended insurance committee hearing in an obscure neck of the state capitol. Several industry representatives testify in support of the industry-written bill. Only a handful of legislators are present. After the hearing, the committee favorably reports the bill.

Two weeks later, after virtually no debate, the bill passes both the House and Senate. Another piece of special interest legislation has made its routine way through the Connecticut General Assembly.

For too long this scenario has summarized what was grandly labeled "the legislative process" — not just in Hartford but in every state capital in the nation. While state legislatures made decisions on important issues, citizen involvement was almost nonexistent. There were no citizen groups tracking legislators' voting records, no groups monitoring committee meetings, and no citizens attending public hearings to express their views.

What this book is about—citizens lobbying in the public interest—is a response to a serious imbalance in our system of government, a system in which special interests often speak with disproportionately loud voices. In theory, the legislature hears all sides of an issue and, after thoughtful deliberation, makes a decision based on the merits of the issue. Instead, economic clout has too often determined government's course of action.

Important decisions by state legislatures on the cost of prescription drugs, the price of electricity, and the regulation of air and water pollution have often been controlled not by the general public whom legislatures supposedly represent but by pharmaceutical companies, utilities, and industrial polluters. These groups have had lobbyists stalking the legislative halls ready to pounce on any legislation that might hurt them. The rest of us have had no one.

Since the early 1970s, growing numbers of citizens have been fighting to correct this imbalance. "Public interest" and "citizen action" groups have been formed in some two dozen states, including Connecticut, where the Connecticut Citizen Action Group (CCAG) began working on consumer and environmental issues in 1971.

Public interest groups have a two-fold goal: to let state officials know that somebody is looking over their shoulders, and to encourage citizens to do that looking, to tell their representatives how they feel and what they want—in short, "accountability." Public officials must be accountable to the citizens who put them in office.

This book describes some of the ways the members and staff of CCAG have tried to accomplish this ambitious goal.

CCAG has been a watchdog—scrutinizing what happens at the legislature by being there when important decisions and meetings take place. Clearly, legislatures effectively represent special interests because they have full-time lobbyists, lawyers, and researchers to present their views—all supported by tremendous economic power. CCAG quickly realized that citizens too need full-time lobbyists, lawyers, and researchers. In fact, citizens need them even more, because they lack the economic power of the special interests. Having full-time paid staff enables a citizen group to carefully monitor the legislature. Perhaps that is why one legislator, giving his constituents a tour of the capitol, pointed to one of CCAG's members and said, "Here's a CCAG lobbyist. They're here to see that we do everything right."

CCAG has placed a high priority on providing information to legislators. Connecticut's legislature, like most others, is part-time and has little staff, which means that legislators depend largely on lobbyists for their information. The job of the citizen lobbyist is to fill the information gap. On any important issue, legislators receive a steady barrage of information from special interests presenting their sides. If a citizen group does not provide counterarguments, no one else will.

By providing thorough and accurate information, CCAG's lobbyists have established themselves as resources for legislators. It is not uncommon for a legislator to ask, "Can you give me some information on this bill? You know more about this issue than I do." Answering this question has been a role of lobbyists for years; what is new is the type of lobbyist and the different perspective.

CCAG has placed equal emphasis on giving information about legislators to the public. Citizens have traditionally lacked detailed information about their state legislators. Local newspapers tend to concentrate on town officials and top national or state politicians. CCAG calls the public's attention to the voting records of their legislators through speaking engagements, press releases, and the annual voting index, which rates legislators on about a dozen roll call votes on key environmental, consumer, open-government, and economic-equity issues. These ratings have made a marked impression on legislators. Some legislators get to be known by their score—"Mr. 11 Percent"—while others half-jokingly warn their colleagues that if they vote against the CCAG position they will get a "minus."

Taking the rating idea one step further, CCAG produced three editions of the massive *General Assembly Project*—four- to eight-page reports on incumbents running for reelection. The information from the reports has shaped campaign issues; incumbents and challengers often quote the profiles in advertisements and press statements. Many newspapers have reproduced the profiles almost verbatim; others have given the reports banner headlines. One paper ran front-page stories on the project five days in a row.

Legislators make it a point to tell the CCAG lobbyist, "I wanted you to know that I missed the vote in committee today because my mother was sick" or "I hope you saw how I voted on that bill. That was the CCAG position, wasn't it?"

Talking to legislators is only part of the story. CCAG's efforts extend far beyond the capitol walls. Throughout the state, CCAG generates and demonstrates public support for its positions. Unlike industry lobbyists, it does not make campaign contributions. It cannot threaten to close a plant in an uncooperative legislator's district. But CCAG can and does educate the public about important issues, and it tells constituents what their legislators are doing in the name of the public and at public expense.

Public awareness gives CCAG its clout. Directly (through lobbying) and indirectly (through teaching other citizens how to generate political pressure), CCAG aims to strengthen that connection between the government and the governed without which representative democracy is jeopardized.

CCAG's experience demonstrates that people *can* affect decisions at the legislature. Through CCAG's achievements, we hope to dispel the cynicism and helplessness many citizens have felt in recent years. The success of CCAG and other citizen groups around the country has shown citizens that they can score impressive and important victories against strong opposition.

What we have begun in Connecticut can be repeated and improved upon where you live. There is nothing unique about what CCAG has done or the experiences it has had. It can be done in your state. We developed skills through on-the-job training in the capitol corridors and late-night drudgery in our cluttered offices. You can too.

Each of the coming years will see an increase in the number of citizen groups across the country as more and more citizens decide to take action to protect their interests. We hope this guide will help you and other citizen activists in that effort.

☆ 1 ☆
A Bill Whose Time Had Come

Pen in hand, Governor Ella Grasso of Connecticut proclaims, "This is an idea whose time has come," and signs into law the state's "bottle bill."

The next day's newspaper carries a photo of the bill's sponsor, together with CCAG's director, both grinning from ear to ear, and a reporter concludes, "Support for the bottle bill was so strong . . . that the measure would have passed if it had required all the empties to be returned to the Capitol rotunda."

The bill had traveled a long way, from the late 1960s, when it was first introduced and was dismissed, to its signing in April 1978. The campaign that made the "bottle bill" law embodied all the important elements of any legislative lobbying effort; it is, for a book on lobbying, a textbook case.

The bottle bill had been around for a long time. A simple idea, it requires deposits on beer and soda containers. Its two primary aims are to curb the tremendous amount of waste when containers are not recycled, and to reduce the litter on streets and highways. It was first introduced in Connecticut by an independent state senator with a reputation for introducing bills that were innovative. The bill faced a powerful array of opponents: bottle and can manufactures, soda bottlers, beer brewers, distributors, retailers, and labor unions.

In 1975 the bill made it out of committee for the first time, but was soundly defeated on the House floor. In 1976, the bill met the same fate in the Senate.

CCAG learned from those defeats. In the summer of 1976 a statewide coalition of staunch bottle bill supporters met with the bill's chief legislative backer, a politically savvy Republican who had taken on the bottle bill as his own cause. The strategy developed was simple: Aim at those legislators most likely to change their minds, and organize constituents in their districts. Diehard opponents (such as legislators who had bottling plants in their districts) were written off. Five categories were devised — definitely opposed, leaning against, undecided, leaning toward, and definitely in favor. The categories were assigned cautiously; there was no wishful thinking about where a legislator stood. Only when a legislator's position was confirmed more than once in print, in a newspaper story or a letter to a constituent, was his or her position deemed definite. At any sign of wavering, the legislator was removed from the definite category. The coalition met every two weeks to update the list, exchange information, and plan tactics. (By continually updating our list, we eventually predicted the final vote exactly.)

The 1976 election was coming up and we decided to inject the bottle bill as an issue. We turned to our current *General Assembly Project*, which listed each legislator's vote on the bill in the previous session, and asked their challengers how they intended to vote on the issue. Using this information, coalition members took every opportunity to ask candidates about the bottle bill — thus making it a campaign issue. After the election, we updated our list. Some legislators we had labeled diehard opponents had won by narrow margins, which meant they might view the issue in a different light now.

Meanwhile, we broadened the coalition to include fish-and-game clubs, homeowners' associations, civic associations, and other groups not previously connected with the issue. By the time the bill passed in 1978 more than 500 groups had endorsed it.

Coalition members were not just names on a letterhead. They participated in massive letter-writing and telephone campaigns. They were joined by the CCAG Citizen Lobby, a telephone network of citizens around the state. Before key votes, when our lobbyists felt that certain legislators needed shoring-up or that a last-minute effort might bring someone into the "yes" column, the citizen lobby telephone network for those districts was set in motion.

In some cases our action was more direct. At one point, the bill hit a parliamentary roadblock and we needed the signature of one last senator on a petition. The hold-out senator woke up at 7 a.m. on the day the petition was due — a Saturday — to see a delegation of citizen lobbyists assembled on his lawn. The senator succumbed and signed the petition at a highway rendezvous with the bill's Senate sponsor, who then drove the 80 miles to the capitol to submit the petition 15 minutes under the wire.

As the campaign began in earnest in the summer and fall of 1977, we updated our research on the issue. We already had research to back us up, but we sought additional ammunition to counter the opposition. We conducted a price survey showing that soda in returnable bottles cost less than soda in throwaway containers. We tackled the jobs issue head-on, emphasizing a Department of Environmental Protection report showing that more jobs would be created than lost by the bottle bill. We compiled information from Vermont and Oregon — states that had already implemented deposit laws — showing that the effect on jobs had been negligible and litter had been drastically reduced. We published figures documenting the limited amount of landfill space to dramatize the absurdity of filling that scarce space with bottles and cans used only once. We took advantage of information leaked to us by sympathizers within the industry, using it to get a head start in countering new arguments. We prepared fact sheets with easily understandable information for citizens to use in lobbying their legislators.

Momentum for the bill began to build even before the 1977 legislative session started. The press was crucial to the success of the campaign, publishing reports on legislators' positions, giving good coverage to the many press releases issued by coalition members, and generally keeping the issue in the public eye. CCAG paid very special attention to the press and used every possible opportunity to garner press coverage. Most of the coverage that was generated centered on activities at the legislature. At the public hearing in 1977 we came prepared, not for the committee members who had heard most of the arguments and statistics before, but for the press and the public. Instead of merely reciting dry statistics, we brought colorful charts and other tangible exhibits that provided good newspaper and television "copy."

While an industry opponent droned on at one microphone, CCAG's representative began assembling his charts on easels. Like a magnet the charts drew the television cameras and photographers even before the industry opponent stopped speaking. On another occasion, we brought sacks of bottles to the capitol steps with a large poster that demonstrated graphically the vast difference in the bottles' value as scrap glass and their value if the bottle bill were in effect. When industry began pushing hard for its substitute, a litter bill that was a thinly disguised ploy to knock off the bottle bill, we dubbed it a "Trojan Horse." We built a huge cardboard horse, filled it with throwaways, and held a press conference on the capitol steps. At a key moment in the conference, the bottles and cans tumbled out, dramatizing the litter bill as an anti-bottle-bill subterfuge. The Trojan Horse became a minor celebrity and helped to prevent bottle bill supporters from defecting to the litter bill. It was also lots of fun and a great morale booster, something not to be overlooked in a long, hard-fought campaign.

We also used public hearings to show our strength and gain publicity. Evening hearings were held on the bottle bill at several locations around the state. These hearings provided an opportunity for us to show that the bill had statewide grass-roots support. We brought local citizens to the hearings who would have been unable to attend a daytime hearing at the capitol.

While the coalition worked to mobilize citizen support, it also carefully mapped out the strategy to be used to carry the bill through the legislative maze at the capitol. Because the Democrats controlled both houses, we needed important Democratic co-sponsors who would actively push the bill. The House environment committee chairman became a leading spokesman, and the Senate majority leader joined the cause. We ended up with two strong floor managers in each house, one from each party. The majority leader, in particular, proved invaluable in helping to change votes and keep supporters in line. Support was garnered from state agencies — the Department of Environmental Protection, the Energy Division, the Department of Transportation, and the Resource Recovery Authority. This support was not decisive, but it certainly helped: Opposition from these agencies would have made our job harder.

The governor essentially kept her hands off the issue. Although she did issue a statement in favor of the bill late in the 1975 session when it was clear that the bill was doomed, she never actively supported it. According to cynics, she issued the statement sure that the bill would lose. Once it was issued, however, it was impossible for her to back off, especially when it became clear that the majority of the voters backed the measure. Again, her tepid support was not essential, but it meant one less battle to fight.

We made several compromises. We removed penalties from the bill so it would not have to go through the judiciary committee, where we knew we did not have the votes. We agreed to a six-month delay in the bill's effective date in return for a desperately needed last signature on a petition. We also agreed to an amendment guaranteeing compensation to any workers who lost their jobs because of the bill. Although we had no objections to its provisions, the amendment was primarily a strategic maneuver to prevent erosion of support from legislators fearing job losses. The amendment proved invaluable in holding waverers steady and in increasing support. With this amendment, the jobs argument no longer carried much weight. The rule we followed was: "Compromise when you absolutely have to, provided you don't give away very much. When you have the votes, don't compromise."

We underestimated our opponents in 1977. Led by the Senate's ace parliamentarian—who, the joke was, slept with the rule book under his pillow—they succeeded in killing the bill even though it had passed both houses! The *coup de grace* was given via an obscure 20-year-old statute and its interpretation by the Senate president—a bottle bill opponent.

We made a last-ditch attempt to attach the bottle bill as an amendment to the industry-backed litter bill. By that time, however, enough legislators who had previously voted yes abandoned us and voted no, dooming the bill for 1977.

In retrospect, we concluded that the bottle bill had too much "soft" support. Gearing up for the 1978 session, we went after the "soft" supporters in a new way by setting up "accountability sessions"—meetings between a legislator and constituents—in their districts. These meetings extracted commitments to support the bill in 1978. Continued pressure and increasing public support mobilized through the same methods used in 1977, along with the "jobs" amendment, brought some previous opponents into the "yes" column. By the day of the Senate and House votes, the conclusion was foregone. We won by substantial margins in both houses.

For us, it was a stupendous victory and a good example of how organized grass-roots citizen action can defeat the special interests despite their seemingly limitless supply of money and power. After unsuccessful industry-backed attempts to repeal or postpone it, the bottle law took effect in January 1980.

☆ **2** ☆

Groundwork

It's a beautiful spring day, and you decide to take a walk. As you stroll down Main Street, it hits you—something is wrong. You can't quite put your finger on it . . . wait, now you know . . . it's garbage. The town is filthy. Not just any old garbage, but bottles and cans—bottles and cans strewn all around. Budweiser, Coke, and Yoo-Hoo look up at you from the gutter. "What a mess," you think. "When I was a kid, I used to bring empty bottles back to the store and get money for them. Now they're just thrown all over." Disgusted, you return home.

You reach into the refrigerator for a can of something cold and head for a chair. As you wrestle with the pull—tab, you notice the price stamped on the can. Sigh. You pick up the newspaper, desperate for some good news. You scan the front page. Another sigh. Right next to the story about the town landfill running out of space is one about waste. Seems that we use too much energy, that it costs too much and damages the environment. Says here that we have to conserve, to reuse things and not simply throw them away . . . . Yet another sigh: "Why doesn't someone *do* something?"

You are someone. And, presumably, if you are reading this book you *have* decided to *do* something: to lobby for legislation. You have taken a big step.

But before you start figuring out how glad you will be

once this wonderful new law is passed, there are a few details to attend to.

KNOWING YOUR ISSUE

The streets are dirty. Soda and beer cost too much. There is too much garbage. You yearn for the days of your youth.

So what? Before you can convince the state legislature and the governor — or even your friends and neighbors — that requiring deposits on beverage containers will save the world, you will need to know a lot more about the issue.

Is it really a problem? How do you know? Who does it hurt? Who does it benefit? What does it cost? What will it cost to solve? What is the best solution? Is passing a law the best way to solve this problem? *Who cares?* You will have to answer each of these questions and more. The only way to do that is to know the facts before you start talking. Once your lobbying campaign picks up steam you will have time for only tactical research, so you had better do your homework now.

Start at your local library. Use the card catalog to find books on the subject. Locate articles on the issue in magazines and newspapers by consulting sources such as *A Readers' Guide to Periodical Literature* and *The New York Times Index.* To dig much deeper you may have to go to a larger library where you can find such resources as the *Index of Legal Periodicals* and *Public Affairs Information Services,* which list more detailed articles. The *Congressional Quarterly* reports on United States legislative activities. The *Index to Government Documents* is somewhat complicated, but it can lead you to comprehensive reports. The *Federal Register,* published daily by the U.S. government, lists all new, proposed, and amended regulations issued by federal agencies. It does not cover federal *statutes,* (that is, laws) which are bills already enacted. These are compiled in the United States Code. Through a variety of loose-leaf services, such as the *Commerce Clearinghouse Series,* *U.S. Law Week,* and the Bureau of National Affairs loose-leaf service (which includes the *Environmental Reporter,* the *Energy Users' Reporter,* and the *Product Safety and Liability Reporter*), you can follow current developments in special fields. Do not overlook trade and professional journals. These offer useful data and a clear picture of what arguments you can expect from your opponents.

The single most valuable resource in the library, though, is the reference librarian, who can clue you in to indexes, abstracts, interlibrary networks, and other sources you may not know about.

Universities, state agencies, large businesses, and industrial associations often have specialized libraries. Most of these are not open to the public, but a polite telephone request may secure permission for you to use the facilities.

Perhaps the most helpful sources of specialized information are people and groups working on similar issues. Both national and state citizen groups are willing to share information, to add momentum and publicity to matters of common concern.

The appendix of this book lists the Public Interest Research Groups (PIRGs) that have been organized by students in more than two dozen states and Canada. It also gives details about groups (and their publications) that have been formed within the Public Citizen network in Washington, founded by Ralph Nader. One of the most useful publications listed there is *Good Works: A Guide to Social Change Careers,* which describes hundreds of local, statewide, and national organizations. This guide is available for $25.00 from the publisher, The Center for Study of Responsive Law, P. O. Box 19367, Washington, DC 20036. It is a valuable resource for local activists looking for information and assistance.

Be aware of what other states are doing. One of the most effective and widely used lobbying techniques is the citation of similar legislation that has passed or is about to pass in other states. Having such legislation on the books elsewhere makes your proposal respectable and enhances its chances for passage. The reports and reference directories of the Council of State Governments (or its regional conferences), usually available in the library of your state legislature, will keep you abreast of what other legislatures or state agencies are up to. The council publishes a handy pamphlet called "State Administrative Officials, Classified by Functions." State manuals and telephone books from other capital cities may also be available. Writing directly to officials in other states for information usually yields good results. Always try to get copies of relevant bills and testimony.

For more information on research, read *Finding Facts Fast* by Alden Todd (Ten Speed Press, Berkeley, Cal., 1979). It is a readable book that amply fulfills the promise of its title.

ZEROING IN

Once you are familiar with the issue, you should begin to gather information closer to home — adapting what you have learned to your own state. It is fine, for example, to talk about Oregon's very successful bottle bill, which has virtually eleminating throw-away beverage bottles and cans there, but that alone may not be enough to convince skeptics that similar results are possible in your state.

For this phase of your research, you will probably have to use more direct sources. In many cases, the information you want will be unpublished — lying around in state agency files, perhaps, or otherwise not easily available. This means some original research is in order.

State agencies. No matter how hostile a state agency may be to you or your viewpoint, you can still extract information from it. Many states have passed freedom-of-information laws, so if you know what data you need from the agency's files, the agency may have to provide it. Rather than going through these formal channels, however, it is much better to develop a working relationship with friendly staff — not necessarily "whistleblowers" who leak really hot information embarrassing to an agency, but people with whom you can deal regularly and cooperatively. Get to know the people who are receptive.

Academics. Do not forget academia. Look around for activist university people to help you with the more technical aspects of your issue. CCAG, for example, has had its own air pollution expert and its own prescription drug expert—not actually on our staff, but university professors who work regularly with us.

The opposition. The best sources of information—the utilities, the polluters, the landlords, or the drug manufacturers—are not likely to open their files to you. Professional publications or reports to state agencies may reveal some secrets, but many questions may remain unanswered. Try writing letters or telephoning, using just your name and home address rather than your group's name and address if you feel your organization is unlikely to be treated fairly, but be prepared for evasion or no response at all. Again, be friendly; the person dealing with you may then be more willing to help. Being antagonistic will only hurt your effort to get information.

Becoming your own source. If you have the means, you may want to do some in-depth field research. In 1973 we were seeking legislation to permit the advertising of prescription drug prices. Several studies had shown that the price of a prescription drug varies widely from pharmacy to pharmacy but there was no information dealing specifically with Connecticut. So we gathered our own. After a three-year struggle during which we used and updated our original survey, we won not only the advertising bill, but a more important one requiring drugstores to post the prices of commonly prescribed drugs. Second only to passage itself, the most satisfying part of the struggle was having our price surveys quoted authoritatively in the legislative debate.

Using your research wisely. Keep in mind that you are becoming an expert in order to convince key legislators of the justice of your position. Most legislators will not be interested in hearing all the details—but that does not mean you do not have to know them. You will have to know the issue thoroughly for those few key legislators whom you hope to persuade to run with it. And of course, you must be able to counter the opposition's arguments.

In preparing your arguments choose your sources of information carefully. Legislators are more likely to be convinced by a quotation from *Business Week* than by one from the newsletter of a small ad hoc group. Maintain your credibility by sticking to verified facts and accepted sources.

Update your research. While your basic research should be complete before the session begins, you must remain up to date in order to take advantage of and respond to fast-breaking events. Contemporary news clippings on nuclear power plant accidents made utility executives squirm in their seats, and helped pass one of our nuclear power bills.

Do not climb out on unsupported limbs (the counter forces have a raft of saws). Do not pretend to know more than you do. If you have done your homework, what you know will be sufficient and certainly more than what most legislators know about your issue. And when you do not know something, admit it. *Never* guess with a legislator. If you do, you may not be taken seriously again. Instead, promise to get the answer, and then do it. Legislators will forgive your ignorance, and will be impressed by your honesty and diligence.

WRITING THE BILL

> "We have no alternative but to turn down any cockamamie piece of legislation which is going to require us to carry back maple syrup, salad dressing, baby juice, catsup jars, and God only know what else, for a five-cent refund."

This statement from the 1974 bottle bill debate illustrates how important it is to draft legislation well. Even if you know your bill has only a slim chance of passing, be sure it is written precisely. Shoddy draftsmanship gives opponents and potential supporters an easy excuse to oppose a bill, and gives you a reputation for carelessness.

In drafting a bill, you have to aim for universal agreement on its meaning. Then, it is to be hoped debate can focus clearly on the issues you had in mind. Moreover, if your bill becomes law, it will be read, interpreted, and applied by legislators, lawyers, judges, and others—who may be hostile, sympathetic, or indifferent to the goals you had in mind when you drafted the bill. The prescription drug law that we fought for requires that pharmacists disclose price information to any "prospective purchaser" requesting it. We intended this to enable consumers to be told prices over the telephone, but pharmacists interpret "prospective purchaser" to mean someone who comes into the store with prescription in hand. There is a world of difference.

Remember that your opposition's lawyers will look for loopholes; don't make it easier by creating any for them.

How to get a bill written. The easiest way, if you can manage it, is to have a legislator be responsible for drafting the bill. A conscientious legislator who is enthusiastic enough about working on your bill may be willing to have it drafted, but you will still have to work closely with the drafter to make sure the bill says what you want it to.

Few legislators, however, will be willing to get your bill drafted. A perpetual problem for part-time legislators is getting bills written. As a result, many special interest lobbyists are able to step into the breach. You can too. Legislators are much more likely to sponsor bills that are already written. A lawmaker who likes your proposal will be grateful to have a written bill—rather than just an idea—as a starting point.

An attorney's help is important, though not always essential, in drafting a bill. Familiarity with relevant state law is crucial. Statutes from other states can help, too. Several groups, including the American Bar Association, the Council of State Governments, and the American Law Institute, publish collections of model legislation on various issues each year. The Commission of Uniform State Laws produces a similar publication aimed at encouraging consistency in state statutes. Sometimes wording can come from federal statutes and regulations, an unsuccessful bill from a previous session, or a bill from another public interest group.

Some states have bill-drafting manuals. Check with the legislative bill-drafting commission, legislative library, or a friendly legislator.

With these materials as guides, even a nonlawyer can piece together a bill. However, we strongly advise that you show your product to an attorney for advice and assistance in polishing up your draft. Remember that your legislative opponents are likely to be (or have the assistance of) attorneys. If you are going to take the trouble to draft and lobby for a bill, be sure it is a sound one—one that is not easy for the opposition to poke holes in.

Finding an attorney who will assist you, if necessary, is not as difficult as you might expect. In the past few years, increasing numbers of lawyers, especially young ones, have become interested in public interest work. Find out whether conventional law firms in your area have *pro bono* attorneys. (This is legal shorthand for *pro bono publico*, "for the public good," and refers to lawyers who handle public interest cases for free.) You might be lucky enough to have a public interest law firm near you that will help you write legislation. Recent environmental laws have brought forward a wealth of environmental attorneys. Neighborhood legal service centers typically house lawyers concerned with problems of low-income people. Law schools are also fertile ground for sympathetic professors and students.

Whoever drafts your bill, it is a good idea to circulate

copies to allies and other interested groups for comments and suggestions. While you are getting your bill drafted, you should be looking for a sponsor—a legislator to introduce your bill and work actively for it. This means you have to learn how the legislature and the legislators work.

KNOWING THE LEGISLATURE

Legislators

Sizing up legislators can be a long and arduous undertaking. Generally very little information on individual legislators is available in handy form in one place.

Short of publishing your own *General Assembly Project,** what can you do? You can go to some of the same primary sources we used in compiling our profiles, but instead of engaging in a comprehensive research effort, narrow your focus to your own particular issue. A legislative library (or whatever legislative records are kept in your state) is an important resource center. Start with the basics there. Get to know the names of legislative leaders and key committee chairpeople. Check records of past legislative sessions, which may include transcripts of public hearings and floor debates, lists of bills and their sponsors, and records of votes. Many states keep verbatim transcripts of legislative proceedings. Read these to learn the players and the lines of debate on each bill, as well as the various legislators' personalities. Any windbags, clowns, heel-draggers, or parliamentarians spring from the printed page.

The library of the legislature and main libraries in major cities should receive a variety of state newspapers. Capital city papers treat the legislature as a local business and cover it closely. Papers from smaller towns run stories on local legislators and issues. These can give you clues to what is important to a

---

*See *Nobody's Business* by Toby Moffett (Chatham Press, Riverside, Conn., 1973) for a detailed account of the 1972 *General Assembly Project.*

and issues. These can give you clues to what is important to a particular legislator, what will determine whether he or she is reelected by the folks back home. Many libraries have collections of newspaper clippings, filed by legislator, bill, issue, or state agency. Also, try the morgues of local newspapers for files on local legislators and local angles on statewide issues.

Ask other groups for information on legislators. Often such groups as the League of Women Voters, the Civil Liberties Union, and business and industry associations publish newsletters during the legislative session that give information on individual legislators. A local or state political organization may publish ratings of legislators' votes, similar to our *General Assembly Project.*

In sum, read transcripts and news clippings and talk with other individuals and groups to gain valuable insight into the political background of your issue and the people involved.

As you begin to play an active part at the state capitol, as you talk to and observe legislators, reporters, and other lobbyists, you will begin to compile your own legislative profiles in your mind.

These are some of the questions you should answer about the legislators you have determined will be important to your issue:

1. What kind of constituency does the legislator have— rural, urban, suburban? What are the principal influences there—labor, business, farmers?

2. What were the winning margins in his or her previous elections? If they were narrow, the legislator knows he or she is vulnerable.

3. What is his or her background: upbringing, education, wealth, other previous experience?

4. What kind of personality does he or she have? What are the legislator's idiosyncracies?

5. What sort of ties does the legislator have to the state or local party organization?

6. Is he or she respected by other legislators? Does he or she influence others?

7. What does the legislator do when not legislating? If the legislator is an attorney, who are his or her clients? This is very important to know because of potential conflicts of interest.

8. Where do the legislator's campaign contributions come from?

9. Who or what influences this legislator the most?

10. Does the legislator hope for higher political office?

By the time the session begins, you should know who the leaders of each house are, who chairs key committees, and who your major allies and opponents are likely to be. Now is the time to watch them in action.

Nothing important may happen on the floor during the first few days of the session, but it is a good time for you to observe the legislative species in its native chamber. Later in the session you will not have time to sit through an entire afternoon Senate session just to see who's who — so *do it now.* If a seating plan listing legislators' names (or a list with photographs) is available, get one and take it with you to the session. Watch and listen.

Notice that tall woman who commanded a respectful silence when she had the floor. Remember who was speaking when the chamber suddenly emptied. Pay attention to the quiet-looking man in the gray suit who spoke so eloquently on a minor point that you found yourself thinking it was an issue of great import. And note well the legislator in the loud suit who keeps bringing up the same wacky idea, only to be shouted down by his colleagues. Connect faces to names. Who's the majority leader? There, the stocky, gray-haired man in blue. Which one is the environment committee chairman who everyone says is dead set against the bottle bill? This is your cast of characters. Study them well, for you will be spending the next several months trying to figure out whether they will vote for or against your bill.

Staff

A state government employs a great variety of people, from elevator operators to state police, from "go-fers" to counsels. It also harbors a number of other characters, ranging from patronage clerks to interns, from serious lobbyists to cranks. The staff of the Connecticut bill room routinely describes to uninitiated new legislators such extras as the woman who waited in the governor's office all day, every day, for several years, claiming that she owned all the land in the United States and wanted it back.

It is important to be familiar with the physical plant, so get to know the state capitol from coffeepot to lavatory. You should look as if you know where you are going, literally as well as figuratively. Some statehouses offer guided tours; take one. After that, try to take a more political tour—guided by, say, a friendly lobbyist who has been around a session or two. Besides learning where various offices and facilities are, find out which do what and at whose bidding. The House and Senate chambers are the most visible parts of the legislature, but the nitty-gritty work is carried on by staffers working in less august quarters hidden in the wings.

Although their exact titles vary, most state legislatures include the following staff offices (their Connecticut titles are listed in parentheses):

The bill writers (Legislative Commissioners' Office). They not only write bills, but also check bills written by others for language and compatibility with existing statutes. In many states, *all* bills, whoever writes them, have to go through this office.

The researchers (Office of Legislative Research). They do research for individual legislators and committees. They may also issue special reports available to the public.

The money specialists (Office of Fiscal Analysis). They do general budgetary research. They also report on the "fiscal impact" (cost incurred or income produced) of all tax and appropriations bills and, upon request by any legislator, of any other proposal.

The housekeepers (Office of Legislative Management). They administer the legislature: coordinate activities and staff, assign rooms, pay salaries, publish manuals of the legislature's rules, and so forth.

The information givers (Information Room and Bill Room). They provide information on a bill's status—exactly where it is in the legislative process. Many states use computers to keep track of bills; the terminals are located here. The Bill Room distributes copies of bills and daily publications. Personal boxes for regulars at the capitol—organizations, state agencies, officials, and lobbyists—are located here. People who reserve these boxes (on a first-come, first-served basis) receive all new bills and daily publications automatically. If you are going to be a regular, see if your legislature offers this invaluable service.

And get to know these work areas:

House and Senate clerks' offices, where you often can find out what bills and amendments have been filed, before the bills are printed.

Majority and minority leadership offices, where many of the decisions are made. Short of barging in, you can often tell when something is up just by who goes in and out.

Committee rooms, where much of the action, formal and informal, takes place and where you will find your home away from home.

Legislators' work space or offices, and mailboxes. To keep track of what is going on, find out what daily publications your state puts out. In Connecticut we have:

The Bulletin. It lists committee meetings, public hearings, and other events.

The Calendars. They list bills coming up for action in each house.

The Journals. They tell you what each house did the day before. They also include the text of amendments and how each legislator voted. Also see if there are records of committee actions. Many states have periodic indexes listing by subject, by introducer, or by committee, all bills that have been introduced.

The Legislative Process

Although the details may differ from state to state, the general procedure by which a bill becomes law is the same everywhere: A legislator introduces a bill, which is sent to the committee dealing with the bill's subject area; the committee discusses the bill, possibly amending it, perhaps holding public hearings, and then votes the bill down or votes to send it to the full house for action. There the bill is debated; if passed, it is sent to the governor, who signs it into law or vetoes it. The legislature can override a governor's veto with a large enough vote (usually two-thirds).

If it were only that simple! It is not, so you must be sure to know the specific rules that apply in your own state. The following will give you a general idea of what happens—at least, on the surface. We will say more, as we go along, on the happenings beneath the surface.

Introduction of a bill. Bills are introduced by individual legislators or by committees. Twenty-three states have an "initiative" procedure to allow citizens to petition for legislation.

Forty-one states have some deadline for filing of bills, and most states allow (one state requires) presession filing. Be sure you know the deadline for introducing bills. Several states have systems for "skeleton" bills (informally worded statement-of-purpose bills) to be introduced. In this case, the formal, statutory language is drafted later.

Referral to committee. Bills are then referred to committees. This is the first hurdle for a bill. It is relatively simple for legislative leaders to kill a bill by referring it to a committee opposed to it. In Connecticut, the majority leader refers bills to committees. Find out who does it in your state.

Committee action. Some states may require committees to hold public hearings on every bill introduced. If your state does not, you may want to work to get a public hearing.

After any hearings, bills may be consolidated, rewritten, and amended by the committee before it decides whether to send the bill to the full house for action (that is, to "report out" the bill). In rare cases a committee may give a bill an "unfavorable report"—sending it to the full house for action but recommending its defeat. Or the bill may be voted down by the committee, ignored, referred to another committee, or referred to an interim subcommittee for further study. These last three actions are usually polite ways to stop a bill. Amending a bill to weaken its effect is another common procedure. Take note: There is usually a deadline for committee action—all bills not reported out of committee by a certain date expire automatically, unless retrieved in one of the ways described next.

Bypassing the committee. If a bill fails to get out of committee, all is not lost. A legislator can usually "petition out" a bill from a committee by getting a certain number of colleagues to sign a petition. Again, there is usually a deadline for this procedure. Another way out—*if* you have friends in high places—is to wait until the deadline for committee action passes. Most states have some provision for legislative leaders to bring bills to the floor, and your bill could be introduced directly at that time. A more likely way to bypass an unfriendly committee is to attach your bill or parts of it to another bill as an amendment.

Floor action. Most bills go from the committee to the full house for action. If the bill is introduced in only one house, that house must act on it. Then, if it is passed, the bill is sent to the other house, where it starts the committee process all over again. This process consumes precious time. By the time it is over, the session will probably be too. Instead, you should have your bill introduced in *both* houses at the start (this is sometimes referred to as "a unibill" or "companion bills"); both houses can then deal with the bill simultaneously.

Warning: *Both* houses must pass exactly the same bill. If the Senate passes a bottle bill requiring five-cent deposits and the House passes a bill calling for ten-cent deposits, you have *no* deposit and *no* return.

Conference committee. When the two chambers end up with different versions of a bill, a compromise is often reached in a "conference committee," composed of key members of both houses. Watch this step closely; many bills have come out of conference compromised beyond recognition.

Action by the governor. When a bill is passed in identical form by both houses, it is sent to the governor, to be signed or vetoed. In many states, if the governor does not act within a given number of days, the bill becomes law without a signature. In others, failure to sign a bill within a given period of time can constitute a veto. If the governor vetoes the bill, the legislature can try to override the veto. Be careful. In some states, the signing/vetoing procedure gets much more complicated at the end of the legislative session.

Keep a good handle on the timetable for the major steps in the legislative process. These usually follow a schedule established by statute or rule. For example, make sure you know when the session convenes and adjourns, what the deadlines are for introduction, drafting, and reporting of bills, and what the schedule is for floor debates. (Letting the clock run out is another favorite way of killing a bill without having to vote it down.) Know the steps a bill must go through, and become familiar with the quirky terminology. The legislature has its own peculiar lingo, which you will soon pick up and use like a veteran.

Since all legislatures differ in detail, here are some fundamental questions you should answer about your state elgislature—*before* the session starts.

1. How are bills introduced (by legislator, by committee, by initiative?)
2. How often does the legislature meet and for how long?
3. How long is a legislator's term?
4. How are committees structured (joint or separate)?
5. Are committee meetings open to the public and are votes recorded?
6. What is the procedure for public hearings?
7. What are the parliamentary rules?
8. What information is public and how is it obtained?
9. Are party caucuses open to the public?
10. Must lobbyists register and is there a fee? What other requirements apply to you?

There are many pitfalls along the way from introduction of a bill to enactment of a law. Once you learn the rules, you can begin to learn how they are ignored, circumvented, exploited, and sometimes broken.

Finding a sponsor. Finding a sponsor is easy. Finding a

good one, however, is more difficult. Legislators will lend their names to bills they may have no intention of working on, to placate constituents or lobbyists, or to build an impressive list to include in campaign literature ("last session I sponsored bills to . . ."), but that is not what you need. You need a legislator who sponsors your bill because he or she believes it is a good bill, and who is willing to *work* to get it passed. The legislator should also be articulate, well liked, respected, a powerful member of the majority party and, preferably, chairperson of the committee the bill must go through. It is a tall order.

First choices. The first obvious targets to approach are the committee chairpeople under whose jurisdiction your proposal falls, unless you already know that they are adamant opponents of the bill. They may not agree to sponsor your bill, but this first contact is important in enlisting their support in the future. (Remember to try to find sponsors in both the House and the Senate.) If you can get a committee chairperson to actively sponsor your bill, you are almost assured the bill will be reported favorably out of committee.

Arrange an appointment as far in advance of the session as possible, and go prepared with drafted legislation and supporting documents—including an explanatory memo and perhaps a few relevant clippings. (Do not drown legislators with paper; if your briefcase bulges, you have brought too much.) Begin with the basics; remember, not too long ago you did not know much about the issue yourself. Construct logical arguments that lead to the conclusions embodied in your legislative proposal. Invite questions, and offer to answer later any that you cannot answer on the spot. Do *not* guess at an answer. This first meeting is a time to size up the outlook and priorities of the chairperson. Politicians are often fickle. Do not assume that the activist of a few years ago, when she was first elected, will jump at your idea. Now that she chairs an important committee, you may find your proposal being scrutinized by a legislator more determined to be "responsible" than "radical."

Any number of responses are possible, from a cold shoulder to a noncommittal murmur to an invitation to become a *de facto* staff member (thus to share resources, and potentially pet issues, with the committee). The most pleasant surprise, of course, is to discover that the committee chairperson has already drafted legislation covering exactly your issue. With luck and hard work, your influence may help make this the best possible legislation.

Second choices. Some committee heads are happy to introduce suggested bills; many prefer not to. Chances are you will have to look elsewhere, so you should be prepared ahead of time with a list of prospective sponsors. A good place to start is with lawmakers who introduced similar but unsuccessful legislation in past sessions, although previous sponsors are not always interested in making a second try. If they are, be sure to find out how the sponsor handled the bill before; you do not want to trust your bill to someone who will be ineffective.

If the issue is new, finding a sponsor requires more effort. Learn which legislators are interested in which issues by checking the bills introduced before the session opens. Using your previous research, you should be able to draw up a list of possibilities in descending order of influence. Members of the majority party who sit on the proper committees and who are respected because of seniority or accomplishments are your best bets for eventual success.

If you have little information on legislators, take a common-sense approach in selecting prospective sponsors. Sell them the issue on its popularity, or appeal to a particular set of their constituents. A legislator from a rural area will not be very interested in a bill for harrassed city commuters. A legislator living near a nuclear power plant may be more receptive to an anti-nuclear-power bill than a lawmaker who lives a hundred miles from the nearest plant.

Line up your sponsors early. Before the session begins is the best time, because then legislators have more time available. A relaxed, unhurried atmosphere is more conducive to presenting a persuasive case for your legislation.

Once someone agrees to introduce your bills, you may think you can relax, at least temporarily. But you cannot. Make sure that the sponsor carries out his or her pledge. Check with the bill-drafting office and the bill room and be prepared to assist your introducer if the bill does not surface.

At the time, finding sponsors may seem to be a major accomplishment. But it is only a very small first step. Finding a sponsor is easy compared with what lies ahead—gathering your forces in support of your bill.

To overcome legislative barricades, you have to understand the myriad forces that influence legislators—the subject of the next chapter.

SUMMARY

1.   *Know the facts before you speak. Back up your statements with solid research.*

2.   *When you do not know the answer to a question, say so. Do not guess. Find the answer and get back to the person who asked the question.*

3.   *Adapt your research to your state's problems and needs.*

4.   *Do not overwhelm with minutiae. State your case in general terms, but be prepared to answer probing technical questions.*

5.   *Write the bill—or have it written—in the clearest, least ambiguous language possible.*

6.   *Try to convince a legislator to get the bill written; then work with the person doing the drafting to be sure the bill says what you intend.*

7.   *For models, look at legislation that has been drafted elsewhere.*

8.   *Get to know as much about the legislators as possible.*

9.   *Get to know the staff of the legislature. Many of them have great influence over your bill.*

10.   *Get to know the legislative rules* before *the session.*

11.   *Look for a sponsor* before *the session.*

12.   *Your ideal sponsor is a legislator who (a) strongly supports your bill, (b) is on the committee that will hear your proposal, and (c) is the powerful chairperson of that committee. Start with (a); aim for all three.*

☆ **3** ☆
Forces

THE LOBBYISTS

Late one night a tired Senate defeats a utility-backed bill to allow burning of polluting high-sulfur fuel. The vote is a victory for environmentalists and an unexpected defeat for the utilities. The next morning a senator known to be a friend of the utilities stands surrounded by five utility lobbyists in varying postures of earnest persuasion. When the Senate is called into session, the senator—who the day before had voted against the utility position—moves to bring the bill back to the floor for another vote.

The senator says later, "There are some things you just have to do."

It is not unusual for a legislator to be heavily influenced by corporate lobbyists. It is unusual for a legislator to completely reverse position so suddenly and publicly.

The Visible and the Invisible

Perhaps you envision yourself, the citizen lobbyist, vying publicly with the corporate lobbyist for a legislator's vote. This does happen sometimes, at committee meetings and hearings and in the halls of the capitol. But not often.

Many lobbyists work behind the scenes. You will not often see them attending committee meetings or buttonholing legislators in the lobby. They have their own meeting places and their own contacts with influential legislators. Many are former legislators who know the legislature inside out and do not hesitate to call on old friends and former colleagues for favors. In the world of special interests, the best lobbyists are the invisible ones. Part of your job is to force them out into the open.

In 1968, when the Connecticut bottle bill struggle began, industry lobbyists were unseen. In 1975, when the bill emerged from committee for the first time, lobbyists for bottle and can manufacturers, soda and beer distributors and retailers— some from out of state—could be seen daily in the halls of the capitol. They were worried enough to bring in workers from local plants, workers whose jobs the industry claimed would be lost if the bill passed. There were rumors about beer and soda being stocked in the Senate caucus refrigerator, anonymous gifts of cases of beer and fruit baskets, and outright cash exchanges. One story told of an attractive blond being pressed upon a particularly stubborn legislator. The success of the pro-bottle-bill lobby had ruffled the special interest lobbyists enough to force them to abandon their usual smooth ways for cruder tactics.

How do special interest lobbyists work, why are they so influential, and how should you, as a different breed of lobbyist, deal with them? The traditional special interest lobbyists are the most plentiful "outsiders" on the capitol scene, sometimes outnumbering legislators almost three to one. Lobbyists come in many degrees of sophistication—from the hard-sell examples, above, to the smooth-talking real estate lobby—and from every imaginable special interest—from the burial vault manufacturer to the podiatrist, from United Airlines to Campbell Soup. Professional lobbyists often wear several hats. One Connecticut lobbyist represented the state's major electric and water utilities, several newspapers, the bar association, a drug manufacturer, and a national oil company.

Wining and Dining

Many people envision lobbyists as cartoon figures— bloated, cigar-smoking villains spreading their pernicious influence by entertaining legislators with wine, food, and women, while occasionally slipping an envelope of money under the table in exchange for a vote. Wining and dining certainly occurs outright, monetary bribes are less evident and probably fairly infrequent. It is a rare legislator who will sell a vote for a meal. Wining and dining, however, provides a relaxed, informal social setting in which lobbyists and lawmakers can get to know each other, exchange pleasantries, and, seemingly incidentally, talk about the host's legislative concerns. The wined and dined legislator does not consciously feel obligated for the free meal; instead, a personal relationship between lobbyist and legislator is nourished at the dining table and the process of friendly persuasion is often oiled at the bar.

A Brotherhood of Interests

"We hear from the highway lobby, but we don't have to. We are all cousins."

This statement, from a congressional chairman of the committee concerned with highway construction, makes the point: The most effective lobbyists are those who have a close relationship with legislators, whose interests naturally coincide with the legislators' interests or who can persuade legislators that their interests are the same. Long acquaintances made through political parties, business dealings, or social activities are the keystone of quiet, effective lobbying.

Especially with a part-time legislature—which typically consists mainly of real estate agents, lawyers, insurance brokers, and other self-employed people who can afford to take time to work in the legislature—you will find a brotherhood of interests. The insurance lobbyist may be a senator's business colleague, the highway builders the buyers of another senator's cement. One of the most vociferous prohighway legislators in Connecticut needed no convincing by professional lobbyists. He was a sales representative for a large cement company.

"Let's Ask the Experts"

Even the purest-minded legislators often end up sounding like industry representatives for the simple reason that that is who they get their information from. The typical legislator, when confronted with an unfamiliar technical issue, wants to know, "Who is an expert on this? Who can answer my questions?" Too often, the only ones waiting to supply the answers are the paid representatives of the very industry affected by the legislation. "I got more information from lobbyists than I did from the legislature itself," said one legislator.

As a former chairman of the Connecticut General Assembly environment committee put it:

> "When the session started, I didn't know anything about it [the issue] at all . . . I did spend quite a bit of time learning what it was all about from Northeast Utilities people . . . I bought their point of view, no question about that. It was not a question of pressure or arm twisting."

Learning from the Pros

Is there anything to be learned from watching special interest lobbyists? While some of their tactics, such as bribery and excessive entertaining, should of course be avoided, other practices could well be copied by public interest lobbyists. First, the special interest lobbyists are there (either physically or via very frequent telephone calls) at the capitol at every stage of the legislative process, from the introduction of a bill to final passage and beyond. Whether behind the scenes or working the halls and lobbies, they are there. Legislators *know* they are there. And you must be there too, if you have any hopes of countering their efforts.

You have to match their efforts with your own. In 1975 the Connecticut bottle bill was defeated largely due to industry's misleading exploitation of the jobs issue. A legislator whose district contained the major bottle manufacturing plant in the state told of a worker who came to his house with his two small children to urge him to vote against the bill: "With those big brown eyes staring at me, how could I tell their daddy I would vote to eliminate his job?"

Cultivating Friendships

Special interest lobbyists identify and cultivate their natural allies in the legislature, and so should you. Try to make friends. Buying a legislator lunch is not wise, but there is nothing wrong with eating together. If there is a cafeteria or dining area in or near your state capitol that legislators frequent, try to eat there regularly. There is nothing wrong about sharing a table with a legislator. A cafeteria is one of the best places for lobbying, with its relaxed atmosphere.

It is important to maintain a friendly relationship with legislators. While hearty back-slapping may go too far, exchanging pleasantries, jokes, and small talk does much to further a friendship.

Unholy Alliances, or Strange Bedfellows

How should the citizen lobbyist treat the traditional bad guys, the special interest lobbyists? Your natural tendency may be to be hostile. Do not be. Save your energy for arguments on the issues. Separate very carefully the person from the issue. Avoid personal antagonisms.

You will find that endless committee hearings, meetings, and floor debates will throw you and "them" together. Be friendly. It can pay off in a tidbit of information being provided. Talking with them also gives you an insight into the arguments they will be using to sell their viewpoints. You will be able to sharpen your wits for future discussions with legislators. And be sure to get all their written information and propaganda.

Make it a friendly rivalry, and if by chance you find yourself and your "enemy" on the same side of an issue, do not be afraid to work together.

STATE AGENCIES

State agencies, the administrative branch of state government, exert a tremendous influence on the legislature. Just as lobbyists do, administrative officials fill a vacuum left by the absence of substantial full-time staff.

Most agencies have a legislative program that the relevant committees almost automatically introduce as a courtesy, although the agencies must solicit support and guide the bills through just as lobbyists do. Some state agencies send a representative to explain bills and monitor legislation. This person often serves, in effect, as an extra committee staff member.

Know what the state agency concerned with your issue is doing. If the agency supports your position, work closely with it. A state agency can be your strongest ally—*if* the agency is well regarded by the legislature. Before you link your cause to an agency, try to get a feel for the relations between the agency and the relevant legislative committee. If you sense hostility, beware. If there is a good working relationship, try to use it to your advantage.

If an agency plans to introduce legislation you are interested in, get in at the beginning and work to see that it incorporates your concerns. If you cannot get your bill adopted as an agency bill, at the very least try to get agency support for the bill.

If the agency opposes your position, your job is harder but equally important. You must keep tabs on the agency to counteract its pronouncements—which, unless you refute them, may be taken as gospel. (Even if an agency's official policy differs from your position, you should still be able to find agency staff who are helpful. Be persistent.)

Some agencies are particularly protective of special interests and work in concert with them. In Connecticut (as well as other states and the federal government) the highway lobby often has a close relationship with the Transportation Department. On any day, you can see road builders lunching with commissioners in the department cafeteria. The road builders' periodic dinners, outings, and conventions are always well attended by department personnel. It is one big happy family dedicated to laying cement.

Keep in mind that lobbying does not stop at the capitol steps, but extends across the street and across town into the state office buildings. The special interest lobbyists are there, and you should be too.

PARTY POLITICS

In 1974, amidst skyrocketing electric bills, Connecticut gubernatorial candidate Ella Grasso accused the Public Utilities Commission (PUC) of overcharging consumers, and promised to abolish the commission. When she was elected governor, she submitted a bill abolishing the PUC and creating in its place a Public Utilities Control Authority (PUCA). Many in her own party were unhappy with the bill, which failed to address the practice of allowing utilities to automatically pass on increased costs of fuel used to generate power. The PUCA seemed little different from the PUC. The Republicans called it a move to "replace our cronies with your cronies."

The governor ordered House and Senate leaders to oppose all amendments to the final version of the bill. Discontent among senators was so great that the public was barred from the previously open Senate caucus in anticipation of a bitter debate.

The governor pulled out all the stops. Her prestige was on the line. She was afraid that if a full, open debate was allowed, the bill would be defeated. We had convinced a freshman representative to introduce an amendment eliminating a particularly bad clause from the bill. Within minutes after he began seeking support from his colleagues, he was called into the governor's office where the governor, Democratic leaders, committee chairpeople, and utility lobbyists pleaded with him to withdraw his amendment. He did, and when another legislator introduced the amendment he spoke against it. The governor got her way. The bill went through and her campaign promise was fulfilled.

How was the governor able to force recalcitrant lawmakers to vote the way she wished? What went on in the Senate caucus to put down the rebellion? The governor's strength lies in her position as party leader. One can imagine the pleadings in the caucus: "the governor really wants this; you owe it to her; she's the head of the party and you ran on her ticket; her popularity helped to elect you; this party has treated you well . . ."

Behind the appeal to loyalty is the threat of a withdrawal from party favor. The governor as head of the party controls the all-important "patronage"—state jobs given out by political appointment. Commissioners, deputy commissioners, judges, and a variety of lesser lights in state government owe their jobs to the party in power. Legislators who want to get jobs for their political friends must be in favor with the governor and other party leaders to do so.

The governor also controls to a large extent the implementation of public works construction projects. Although the legislature must first authorize issuance of bonds for such projects, the governor decides whether the money is spent and what the priorities are. A legislator who wants a project in his or her district badly enough will hesitate to step out of line.

The governor has a wide choice of ways to punish rebellious legislators. A vast array of state agencies and party officials stand ready to do his or her bidding. It is not uncommon at election time for a legislator who has bucked the governor to find the state party has decided the legislator's race is not as important as other races and therefore entitled to less of the party campaign chest. Or a state senator who initiates an investigation of a state agency against the wishes of the party powers may find that he has lost his committee chairmanship. On the other hand, if a legislator needs extra help in district affairs from a state agency, a good relationship with the governor can be helpful.

Most state legislators have, at best, a few staff members and some party committee members from the district. (Even a governor with a relatively weak hold over the state party structure has more power than any except the most powerful legislative leaders.) The governor sets the budget, and perhaps more important, the governor commands public attention. Some states have over 200 legislators; there is only one governor. When the governor speaks, it is news.

Complementing the governor's power is that of the House and Senate leadership, which has its own system of rewards and punishments to control the rank and file. The speaker of the House, the Senate president, and the House and Senate majority leaders are at the top of the leadership hierarchy, followed by an assortment of deputy and assistant leaders. Lawmakers can get away with stepping out of line occasionally, but if they do it too often, they may find themselves unable to get any bills passed.

Rewards

For the party faithful, there are rewards—a committee chair, placement of a friend in a state job, and best of all, a piece of "pork" from the legendary "pork barrel" to bring back home to the folks. The pork may be a road, a school, a state office building, or anything else that the legislator can point to as evidence of service to the district. (Whether these projects ever get built is another story. Connecticut's legislature has "overauthorized" these types of projects precisely because they are so politically appealing.)

The first rule new legislators are taught is: "To get along, go along." Some mavericks are respected by the rank-and-file, but many are scorned for being ineffective. The most-admired legislators are those who get things done, who use compromise, persuasion, and conciliation to achieve their ends.

Local Politicos

The party game continues on the local level. Legislators may be beholden to a big-city political boss or the local party machinery for their election. If that is the case, they will represent the interests of the local big shots.

Using the Party Forces

The governor, the legislative leadership, the party leadership (sometimes synonymous with the former) both state and local—all are important forces influencing lawmakers' votes. As a citizen lobbyist you should know as much as possible about the intricacies of the party scene. The more you know, the better you will be able to devise tactics and strategy to push through your legislation. Find out who is chummy with whom, who has had a rift with the governor, who supported whom in previous primaries, what the party factions are, who the rising stars may be. Talk with reporters, staff people, and legislators at the capitol, and keep up with local newspaper accounts of party doings.

A legislator may not listen to you, but may listen to someone who helped get him or her elected or who is in a position to do a favor. As for the governor and the legislative leadership, CCAG meets with both (if not the governor, then an aide) at the beginning of each session to discuss legislative priorities. And it does not stop there. You should attempt to develop a working relationship with the governor's office and the House and Senate leaders so that throughout the session you are continually touching base as your bills wind their way through the legislative maze.

THE BAD, THE BEST, AND THE BRIGHTEST

In addition to the formal leaders, there are other legislators who strongly influence their colleagues. Some do so because of the strength of their personalities, some because of their knowledge, some because they are seen as rising stars who will soon be in leadership positions, some because they know how to deal with their colleagues' tender egos. Abrasive, cocky, noisy legislators rarely have much influence.

We found one very good measure of who is respected and who is ignored. When certain legislators rise to speak in floor debate, the decibel level in the crowded chamber will rise as well; when others stand, the chamber will quiet down.

In your lobbying efforts concentrate on those people good for more than their own votes.

Watch for logrolling, the practice of trading votes—"If you vote for my bill, I'll vote for yours." This is a common practice; legislators are reluctant to cross each other, and they like to pay their debts. So, keep your ears perked, and file away any tidbits you hear about vote-traders. You may be able to use them to your advantage.

THE CLIMATE

In the waning days of the 1977 session, the Connecticut legislature passed two important "good government" bills. One slapped tougher regulations on lobbyists, the other set up a citizens' ethics commission to oversee the conduct of public officials. Although there was no heavy lobbying for the bills by masses of ordinary citizens, legislators dared not vote against them. Why?

The time was ripe for such legislation. The political climate created by Watergate—the intense distrust of politicians—guaranteed little or no open opposition to the measures. Once the bills reached the floor they were guaranteed to pass, and we had been careful to ensure that the bills survived the back-room struggles to reach that point.

We were paid a back-handed compliment by one of the few legislators who voted against the lobbying bill. He complained that his constituents did not care about the bill but that it was just fashionable to vote for it:

> "You know they did it in Washington, they have done it in several other states. CCAG wants it. Common Cause wants it. The League of Women Voters wants it."

As a public interest lobbyist you should be aware of the political climate, assess it, and plan your strategy accordingly. We were able to use the public's extreme distrust of government and the politicians' sensitivity to that distrust to get these two important bills passed with fairly little effort.

THE PEOPLE: THE ULTIMATE LOBBYISTS

Politicians want to be reelected. That simple truth explains why the people back in the home district are potentially the most important force influencing a legislator.

Just how much pressure from back home it takes to determine a legislator's vote depends on the issue. Legislators hear nothing from their constituents on the vast majority of bills. When they do get a few letters or telephone calls they take notice. Sometimes a handful of calls can change a vote. On a controversial issue, much more is needed.

Connecticut environmentalists learned their lesson well after two defeats of the bottle bill, and began a massive letter-writing and telephone-calling campaign. Legislators were overwhelmed, and many admitted their minds had been changed by their constituents. Enough had their minds changed to eventually pass the bill.

Grass-roots action or reaction on legislation is not always focused. It may have to be organized and directed.

The next chapter discusses how to do just that.

SUMMARY

1. *Lobbyists come in all shapes, sizes, and colors.*
2. *Monitor the legislative process from start to finish.*

3. *Maintain good relations with legislators and their staff.*

4. *Do not be antagonistic toward opposition lobbyists.*

5. *Know the goals of state agencies.*

6. *Consider the impact of party politics in forming your strategy.*

7. *When possible use the governor to influence legislators.*

8. *Know the interests of the formal and informal legislative leaders.*

9. *Evaluate the climate and pace of the legislature when selecting tactics.*

10. *Never underestimate the influence a constituent has with a legislator.*

☆ **4** ☆
Organizing Support for Your Issues

Waiting in the committee room for the vote on your bill that requires the licensing of nursing homes, you are confident that you have marshaled the most convincing arguments possible. You know you have done sound research documenting widespread abuses in the nursing-home industry. Leading experts have testified for the bill. The facts are clear.

The vote is tallied. The bill has been tabled by a 9 to 6 vote. While you are dazedly wondering how those nine legislators could ignore your convincing evidence, someone points out that your organization has not tapped its members in their districts.

You will not require many such experiences to discover that few bills, if any, pass solely on their merits. Evidence is nice, but facts do not vote; constituents do. *Organizing citizen support for a bill is the most crucial part of lobbying.*

Any serious public interest lobby must have influence *outside* the legislature in order to bring pressure *inside* the legislature. Otherwise, the group risks relying on a handful of friendly legislators to push through all its bills. Most politicians are motivated more by mobilized public pressure and the fear of losing elections than by a desire to maintain friendly ties with public interest groups. And how can your organization be taken seriously as a "public interest" group if there is no visible public supporting what you claim is in their interest?

Building a citizen action organization takes time—a scarce commodity in public interest work. You may decide to forego a major organizing effort during your first try at the legislature. You may choose, for example, to work only as an advocacy group with little grass-roots support—relying on your research abilities, a reputation for acting in the public interest, or your success in drawing attention to your issues in the press. A small staff may force you into such a conventional advocacy role.

But if you want to create a lasting political force for social change you need to build an organization of active citizens to back you up. Though you will have to invest a major amount of time to do this, your organization will ultimately bank the dividends in many more victories at the capitol.

How do you find citizens to organize? How do you effectively combine lobbying at the capitol with constituent pressure? How do you harness the energy of all those citizens who might act if they knew what was going on? How can you get information to people so they know if their legislators truly represent their interests?

The purpose of this chapter is to address these questions. We are suggesting several models—CCAG's own citizen lobby, coalition building, and community organizing. These are some possible approaches for getting citizens involved, but not the only methods or the last word in citizen action techniques. They have worked for us. But the point should be clear—to win on most issues and build effective citizen organizations for the future, you need to build a grass-roots base.

A MODEL FOR DEVELOPING CITIZEN CLOUT: THE CITIZEN LOBBY

"What this country needs is not the good five-cent cigar of time-worn legend, but rather a few million more political activists. . . The political leaders

need to feel the power of the voters who elected
them—the impact of opinion from the grass roots—
to balance the tremendous pressures which are
applied through the well-heeled interests whose
lobbyists haunt the legislative halls."

—*Shoreline Times* editorial
Guilford, Conn.

The political activists are out there—as close as the nearest
telephone. Many of them are waiting for the opportunity to
get involved in their government, but they lack information
on the issues, the skills to participate in the political process,
and someone to convince them that they can make a difference.
One telephone call from you can change all that. A few more
calls and meetings can get those citizen activists talking and
working together. Slowly but surely you can build a grass-
roots network of citizen lobbyists who can be mobilized instantly
to contact their legislators on important bills, and whose
influence can make the difference between winning and losing.

The CCAG Citizen Lobby is just that—a statewide network
of groups and individuals organized to generate telephone
calls, letters, and telegrams, and to appear at the capitol on
short notice. Such a network can also be organized on a smaller
scale, concentrating on a particular town or district. But the
basics of building each citizen lobby are the same. Citizens
who are willing to work on your issues must be identified.
They must be given information on the issues and taught
lobbying skills. And a method must be devised to activate
them quickly when their lobbying efforts are needed.

Our 2,000 citizen lobby members regularly receive
information on legislation that CCAG supports. During the
session, when we learn that a priority issue is about to be voted
on, either in committee or on the floor, the alert goes out over
a "telephone tree" to our local citizen lobbyists. A telephone
tree is simply a network of citizens that transmits information.
Picture a pine tree with a lobbyist at the top. The lobbyist

learns a bill may not have the votes it needs to pass, and contacts five citizens, who each have the names of five others. Each person receives suggestions on what can be done to save the bill—call a legislator, write to him, visit him—and acts accordingly, meanwhile passing along instructions to five other citizens.

By coordinating our efforts at the capitol with constituent pressure on the local level, we are able to demonstrate maximum support for our issues in the legislature. This lobbying strategy is potentially the most powerful weapon of any citizen organization.

Organizing The Lobby

Identifying people who will become your citizen lobby. The audience that you attract depends on the issues you support. Take a step back and analyze your issues. Are there people or organizations in your community who are likely to support your position on them? If there are, how can you convince them that your organization will help them?

At CCAG we began building the citizen lobby by dividing the state into 22 regions, using as a guide the major population areas and toll-free calling zones. The legislature helped us determine what regions would be organized first. We started with the districts of those legislators who chaired committees that regularly handled our legislation. In each region we contacted environmental groups, attended their meetings, and spoke of a network that would link the organizations in a unified legislative lobby. We identified at least one "regional coordinator"—responsible for mobilizing 25 citizens in his or her region. Each of those 25 was responsible for mobilizing 5 or more people, making the minimum quota for each region approximately 125 citizens.

Building the lobby membership. When recruiting people for our citizen lobby we stressed its loose structure: an organization to coordinate letter writing and phone calling, with one optional meeting each legislative session, no weekly or monthly meetings, and no membership dues. We pointed out that the informal nature of the lobby doesn't detract from its effectiveness, or from the excitement of working on a regular basis with other citizens on legislative issues.

As you might imagine, the effectiveness of the citizen lobby model hinges on the performance of the regional coordinators. Ideally, the coordinators should have some experience in the political process, and the enthusiasm and time to hold together a strong local network. One of their most important tasks, for example, is to check with members of their local lobby to determine if all the calls are being made and to identify and patch weak links in the phone tree system.

Building an effective citizen lobby is a continual process. It does not end after the initial organizing effort. It never ends. If it does, the citizen lobby ends too.

Be alert to unexpected recruitment opportunities. At one town meeting organized by a CCAG lobby member, for example, a legislator on the environment committee, who had earlier that day hurled insults at CCAG's director at the capitol, praised our work and thanked everyone for coming. His mood darkened, however, when we politely informed the audience that the distinguished senator had not voted as an environmental advocate during his tenure on the committee and that his private employment might be a conflict of interest. Everyone attending joined the lobby, anxious to be kept informed of their legislator's performance.

Do not wait for invitations to speak to organizations. Contact local women's clubs, civic and community associations, labor unions, and any other relevant groups. Offer to speak about your organization and its issues, stressing the citizen lobby as a means of working together effectively on issues of common concern. When you talk to these groups, cite your successes. (If you are just starting out, cite similar groups' successes.) Such success stories breed enthusiasm and provide strong positive models of effective citizen action.

To build an effective lobby you must also be sure that there is ample opportunity for lobby members to give their ideas on proposed legislation. Your local lobbyists must feel that they are an integral part of the lobbying effort. Citizen lobby members must participate in determining priorities and shaping legislative strategies. If they do not feel part of the decision-making process their interest will be short lived. The military model of orders filtering down to the troops just will not do if you want to attract and keep lobby members.

Need for a citizen lobby coordinator. It is obvious that organizing the lobby and maintaining it require time. At CCAG we have one staff member who works full time building and directing the activities of the citizen lobby before and during the legislative session. Along with building the lobby membership, she is responsible for giving regional coordinators up-to-date information on legislation and lobbying tactics, and activating the regional coordinators and their networks when needed. She also facilitates a constant flow of information between CCAG staff and lobby members on the positions of local legislators.

The statewide coordinator must be familiar with each issue your organization supports; he or she will have to answer questions on all of them.

The coordinator must work in two worlds at one time, being aware of what is going on at the capitol *and* remaining in constant touch with lobby members across the state. He or she will have to travel frequently, prepare mailings, and make and respond to member telephone calls.

How the lobby works: providing information and skills to lobby members. Before the legislative session, we send questionnaires to citizen lobby members on various issues. We also try to hold meetings throughout the state to tap their concerns, establish personal contact, and build enthusiasm.

The questionnaires and local meetings allow us to make

very direct and personal contact with members. We hear about high prices, the unscrupulous ways of some health professionals, the trouble with local mechanics and local polluters, and an endless series of other frustrations. To deal with these concerns we present legislative possibilities — bills on our agenda that might meet their specific needs or interests (or additional bills we might add). As interest is generated, we share insights about local legislators and their positions on issues, and talk about our hopes for the upcoming legislative session.

Another key element of an effective lobby is teaching lobbying skills. To do this we distribute our *Citizen Lobby Handbook* to civic organizations and schools. It includes basic information on state government, including a description of how a bill becomes law, a glossary of legislative terms and rules, a list of party leaders, committee chairpeople, committee action deadlines, a map of House and Senate districts, a map of the state capitol, and a list of legislators, complete with addresses and telephone numbers. The handbook has proved quite useful. (The Center for Study of Responsive Law offers citizens *The Congress Project Profile Kit*, which can be adapted for use at the state level.)

One citizen lobbyist said she understood the legislative process and rules better than her local legislator. The handbook is also a citizen primer on basic lobbying techniques — planning meetings with legislators, writing effective letters, lobbying by telephone, using local media, and so forth.

After this initial briefing we provide our citizen lobby members with detailed information on proposed legislation. We supplement this throughout the session with monthly bulletins on amendments or any other pertinent legislative maneuvers.

In addition to giving the lobby members basic information outlining each bill, we try to anticipate the arguments and questions they can expect to hear from their legislators, and we provide facts to refute opposition statements. Although the arguments and refutations may be familiar to legislators—who will often hear them from your lobbyists at the capitol—they will frequently give the same information more consideration and legitimacy when they hear it from a constituent.

If you are a multi-issue organization, there are likely to be times when your local lobbyists will have mixed feelings about supporting some of your legislation. For example, one regional coordinator's husband worked at a bottling plant. She was interested in consumer legislation, but not in the bottle bill, one of our priority bills. We eventually had to swallow hard, say we understood, and agree to call on her the next time some important consumer legislation came up. We now anticipate these occasional disagreements. When they occur, we simply loop around the missing link. Either the prior person in the telephone tree or the coordinator steps in to make the calls that would otherwise go unmade.

We urge our citizen lobby members to work only on the legislation with which they are comfortable. If you sense that your lobbyists are not committed to a particular issue, do not insist that they go through the motions. If you pressure them, you run the risk of wasting their time and diluting their commitment. Keep records of the issues in which certain lobbyists and coordinators are particularly interested—or uninterested.

Activating the Lobby

After your lobbyists have been organized, have received a description of the issues, and are well briefed on how the legislature works, the citizen lobby should be ready for its initial test.

The first alert may come early in the session, with a key public hearing or a crucial committee vote. When the alert comes the staff notifies lobby coordinators in the citizen lobby districts, who then activate their local phone trees. The tree concept, with one person making no more than five calls, assures speedy delivery of the message, minimal work for each person, and a quick flood of calls or letters to the legislators.

When a selective alert is called—focusing on specific legislators—only lobby coordinators with members in the key districts are called. The coordinators, who have been briefed on the legislators in their area and their committee assignments, will quickly know which of their lobby members to activate.

Legislators who already support your position are not your top priority for this type of pressure, but *never take supporters for granted.* Bolstering wavering supporters can be as important as convincing the uncommitted.

At the beginning of the session, when the legislative committees are considering bills, you will often activate the citizen lobby to contact committee members or turn people out for a key public hearing. Crowds of sympathizers at hearings are a powerful way to demonstrate to committee members that there is public interest in your legislation, so we urge lobby members to attend important public hearings even if they do not plan to make statements. And remember, an offer of assistance in preparing testimony is often the boost that an enthusiastic citizen lobbyist may need to become an effective spokesperson.

For example, an elderly lobby member had become a noise pollution expert after an airport was built near her home. Afraid to speak at a hearing, she consented to sit alongside a CCAG staff member giving testimony, to help answer legislators' questions. Shaking off her nervousness after the first few queries, the woman wound up demonstrating the use of her soundproof headphones and her specially fitted earphones. Smoothly fielding every question, she received a standing ovation from the crowd.

When legislation moves to the floor, the real crunch begins. It is not unusual for your priority bills to come to the floor for debate and a vote in rapid-fire succession. With this hectic pace at the capitol, you must continually reassess your choice of issues on which to activate the citizen lobby. Can the lobby members be alerted in time? Are they familiar with the issue? Can they apply pressure in the appropriate districts? Is there a more critical issue coming up in a few more days? These are all questions you must answer.

We have found that the best rule of thumb is to use the lobby only when we can give members at least two or three days' advance warning. There are, however, exceptions to that rule. We have had emergency situations requiring activation of the lobby the night before a crucial vote. That is obviously cutting it close, considering that first a small army of area coordinators must be notified, and they must then alert all of their local lobby members. Frantic telephone calls have interrupted many peaceful suppers and quiet evenings.

Using the Lobby Efficiently

Don't mobilize the lobby on highly technical issues. We activated the lobby one to support a bill that most of our members knew little about. The issue was complex and we tried to explain it in hurried telephone conversations. The bill passed, but our lobby members were frustrated and annoyed. If you must turn out lobbyists on such complex issues, give *each* lobbyist a full written explanation.

Push one issue at a time. If a local lobbyist calls his or her legislator and runs down a laundry list of bills that merit support, the call and the information lose their impact. Lobbyists should tackle one issue at a time, allowing more time to discuss the importance of the issue, ask and answer questions, and refute misinformation.

Get back to your lobbyists when the battle is over. Lobbyists who have followed a bill on its journey through the legislature will naturally be interested in its fate. Keep them informed. Even when action on the bill is completed, citizen lobbyists will often be willing to follow up with additional calls and letters praising their legislators or scoring them for bad votes. Compile charts for the lobbyists describing key bills and legislators' positions on them.

Constructing an effective grass-roots lobby takes a long time. CCAG is still working on finding new ways to recruit members, perfect our information distribution service, and strengthen the telephone tree.

Why have we labored so long with this conglomeration of individuals we call our citizen lobby? Because effective use of the lobby has been the key to our success. Legislators know now that there is more to CCAG than a handful of lobbyists.

Elected officials must be made aware that informed citizens are monitoring their performance in their districts, and that those citizens have the ultimate mandate of the ballot box to support or veto a legislator's actions.

The citizen lobby concept—combining the efforts of full-time lobbyists at the capitol with local citizen effort—has unlimited potential. It can be applied on many different levels: in towns or cities, in particular districts, or across the state. Its goal, however, remains the same. Local citizen participation is capable of making the legislature, and the whole government, responsive to the people from whom it derives its power and who it is supposed to represent.

ANOTHER MODEL: THE COALITION

A coalition is simply a group of organizations or individuals working to pursue common interests. Whatever its name or purpose, the coalition uses the power of numbers and the power that consensus from diverse groups can provide.

Advantages. Issues are legitimate in the eyes of legislators —and your supporters—when they have backing from a wide variety of groups and interests. A coalition can change the image of the bottle bill, for example, from simply an ecology issue to a consumer-energy-environment issue, broadening its support among the public and in the legislature.

Coalitions also pool the skills and resources of the groups involved, greatly increasing the resources that can be brought to bear on the issue. The organizations in your coalition may be able to contribute valuable technical, legal, or political expertise to the effort. They also may be able to turn out their members for a hearing, or share the financial burden of an issue campaign.

The diverse people involved in your coalition may also provide new perspectives on the issue. For example, when drafting legislation controlling utility service terminations for our energy coalition, other coalition members alerted us to a new wrinkle: delinquent customers who made substantial payments were having their service shut off in the next few days anyway. As a result, we included a requirement for a new termination notice whenever a customer paid 20 percent or more of his or her back debt to the company.

The news media like coalitions, too. You are much more likely to get publicity for your efforts if a large number of different organizations are involved.

Finally, a successful coalition lays the groundwork for future relationships on other issues—relationships that can pay off time and time again on key legislation.

Disadvantages. If coalitions are so useful, why not form them on every legislative issue? Despite their promise, coalitions have pitfalls. Many organizations, for example, were not formed to storm legislative barricades. Some may be prevented from lobbying because of their tax-exempt status, and others simply prefer to direct their energy elsewhere. Though such groups will not be useless to the coalition, they will undoubtedly play a low-key role.

Appropriate tasks have to be found for the apolitical organizations. Some senior citizen groups, for example, may be reluctant to appear at a public hearing on drug prices, but would be delighted to conduct a survey of prescription prices at local pharmacies.

Reaching agreement on your coalition's position on an issue can be difficult. Some groups may not be ready to compromise; others may want to take the time to poll their members before they commit themselves on any decision. In some cases, this delay in decision-making can cripple a coalition's ability to respond to ever-changing legislative situations.

One solution to this problem is to allow each member group to speak for itself when the coalition cannot reach agreement on a particular point. This policy will work for occasional disagreements, but if they are frequent your coalition will seem less and less like one.

Finally, a workable coalition requires that the public credit for victories be shared — even if some groups worked harder than others. Although you must share the publicity, a coalition may insure that there is a victory.

How to Form a Coalition

If you are working on an issue that you know interests other organizations — even if the reasons for their interest differ from yours — then building a coalition is likely to be an appropriate lobbying strategy.

The first step in organizing a coalition is to recruit interested groups. To identify the groups, start with those that are most directly affected by the issue. If it is a landlord-tenant problem, look to the urban organizations. If it is preservation of a state park, go to local environmental groups. In addition to the usual broad advocacy groups such as the Civil Liberties Union or the League of Women Voters, it is vital that local groups representing those immediately involved in the issue be included. Their local or "street" expertise on the issue is often the most valuable asset of your coalition. Consider other groups — community groups, labor unions, consumer groups — that might be interested in the issue. Identify their self-interests and determine if you can tie them in. If you are fighting for tougher water quality standards, say, approach a labor union with the argument that the tough standards will result in increased construction of sewage plants and thus increased employment.

Always approach groups on *specific* issues; avoid generalized causes. People who support a specific issue do not necessarily support your broader goals. People who live near a polluting factory may want to do something about it without agreeing with your broader environmental concerns.

As you contact each group, try to find one key person who is interested in your issue and capable of following up on it. All your mailings and phone calls should be aimed at that individual; otherwise they will inevitably get lost in the shuffle. He or she should be responsible for passing the information on to the organization, encouraging the membership to act on the issue, and generally acting as a link to the coalition. Ultimately, your contact person may also act as a representative for that group at public hearings and as a spokesperson for local media.

Be careful that communication with the groups in your coalition is not one-way. For legislative questions, you can serve as a useful resource simply by suggesting key legislators and lobbying groups to contact. The other groups may also make suggestions for legislation that your group will want to follow. Update the groups on any late developments on the issues. Collaborate on strategy and seek each other's advice. List all the members of the coalition on its letterhead. Everyone involved must feel part of a joint effort. The coalition is a team and must work like one.

COMMUNITY ORGANIZING

In recent years, CCAG has turned, more and more, to community organizing as the method of involving citizens in its work, including lobbying at the legislature. The organization now has ten chapters scattered around the state. A statewide leadership council composed of representatives of these chapters selects the issues on which CCAG will work.

This effort at building local chapters is not tailored simply to mobilizing citizens around CCAG's legislative program.

Our community organizing aims to involve citizens in group action on those problems they feel strongly about. The members of our local chapters determine what issues they work on and how. Some of these issues must be resolved by the legislature. In those cases, the force of citizen action can be combined with the skills of CCAG's staff lobbyists.

Members of a community concerned about a problem — a housing project, a highway plan, a deteriorating neighborhood — are often as angry at what they believe is their own powerlessness as they are at the problem. The organizer's job is to erase these feelings of powerlessness by focusing group effort on the resolution of one tangible problem. The confidence built in citizens by such victories provides the basis for citizen-initiated action on other issues.

Since the problems most people feel strongest about are in their own neighborhoods, community organizing focuses initially on issues of local concern. These may not be issues requiring legislative action. Local chapters gain confidence and develop internal leadership by successfully tackling simple problems such as getting a traffic sign or repairing street ruts. They then build toward attacking broader community problems and more sophisticated targets such as a state legislature.

For citizens to become committed to working through a community organization, the group must choose issues that:

1. are felt deeply and recognized immediately by citizens
2. can be won and result in tangible benefit to citizens
3. attract a broad range of community members

These criteria must be kept in mind when developing legislative proposals requiring the participation of the local chapters.

Chapter members play a vital role in the lobbying process. They have held numerous "accountability sessions" where they meet with local legislators demanding commitments on CCAG's issues. On "Citizen Lobby Days," hundreds of CCAG members appear in Hartford to personally press the fight for passage of key citizen legislation in the corridors of the capitol. When anyone now asks for whom CCAG speaks, the answer is clearer than ever — the 15,000 CCAG members across the state.

Lobbying Activities by Local Organizations

Local groups can conduct a number of activities that can be an important part of any successful lobbying activity. These include:

1. organizing a telephone tree to bring pressure on local legislators
2. attending hearings en masse
3. conducting petition drives to support legislation
4. holding local accountability sessions

This last method may be the most effective one that local organizations or chapters can employ to influence local legislators. One or more local legislators are invited to a meeting of the local group. Unresponsive legislators thrive on anonymity. When they are forced to face their constituents personally, these legislators find it very difficult to oppose the positions of the local group — and of the larger organization of which it is a part.

These accountability sessions should focus on specific demands. In the first part of the meeting, community residents should present the problem. In the second phase, they should propose legislation that represents the group's solution to the problem. The third part is to get the legislators who are present to respond to the demands of the local citizens. Legislators should be urged to commit themselves not only to support the legislative proposal but to work actively for its passage.

This brief discussion cannot adequately describe the principles and techniques of community organizing. There are numerous groups with extensive experience in the development of community organizations. Some of them have developed training and information centers. A selection of these centers is listed in *Good Works* (described in Chapter 2, "Groundwork"). We suggest you contact any or all of them for further information.

SUMMARY

1. Organizing citizen support for a bill is the most crucial part of lobbying.

2. Identify the people who are likely to support your legislation.

3. Constantly recruit new members for your group.

4. Develop citizen leaders within your group. Training is important.

5. Keep your members informed about the progress of the legislative campaign.

6. Mobilize on familiar issues.

7. Let members of your group know what effect they had at each stage at the campaign.

8. Coalitions are always useful.

9. Community-based organizations can produce an institutionalized presence on legislative issues.

10. Coalition building and community organizing require great patience and creativity.

☆ **5** ☆

The Press

You have just worked for four months on a major report documenting numerous scandals in your state's nursing homes. Your group has poured hundreds of hours of work into the report. You have traced down fact after fact and interviewed scores of people, often working late into the night. You hope the report will initiate a major investigation of nursing homes and result in strong legislation to prevent these kinds of abuses in the future.

Which of the following would you prefer when you finish your report?

A. A paragraph or two in the middle of a page-44 newspaper story about hearings on nursing home legislation, to which no one pays any attention.

B. Headlines in every major daily in the state and several minutes on all the state's television stations, with numerous follow-up stories on the issue and appearances on radio and television talk shows, all emphasizing the need for complete reform of nursing home practices in your state. As a result, the chairperson of the legislature's public health committee calls for immediate hearings on the problem.

The choice is obvious. The press can make or break an issue. That is why we believe this is one of the most important chapters in this book.

WHAT THE PRESS CAN DO FOR YOU

You must educate the public about your issue. A front-page story about your report on lead poisoning in children will alert thousands of people to the importance of that issue. It is by far the quickest way to reach large numbers of people — including lawmakers — on any problem. Lobbying alone rarely passes bills. Legislators want to know that someone besides a lobbyist is concerned about an issue: "If it's such a big problem, how come I haven't seen anything in the papers about it?"

Do not rely on the press as the only way to reach your supporters or potential supporters, but remember that it is an important vehicle when time is short and your other avenues of mobilizing support are limited. An emergency appeal for help on a surprise vote on the state environmental policy act, made through a quick press statement by CCAG, brought numerous calls and telegrams to legislators from environmentalists from across the state.

Those lawmakers who have indicated lukewarm support for a measure may become more ardent when they see their names favorably associated with that issue in a news story or editorial. The more publicity an issue gets, the more willing legislators are to make it their bill and fight for it.

By the same token, unfavorable publicity about a position may diminish lawmakers' support. You want legislators to feel that their positions are closely watched and that opposing your position will get them a lot of adverse publicity.

Most people — and legislators are no exception — want to be with a winner. When legislators see story after story — especially favorable ones — in the newspaper or on television about your issue, they get the impression that everybody else is for this issue and perhaps they ought to join in. This means that you may not want to have all your support come out at once. Instead, you might carefully release notices of additional support for your effort over short intervals. (Political candidates often use this tactic.) If there are ten groups supporting your position, have one group after another put out a statement of support each week for ten weeks, instead of holding a single press conference with all ten groups there. This tactic works best, of course, when the issue or the organizations involved are newsworthy enough to attract coverage of each press conference. After all, ten press conferences that receive no coverage are less effective than one that receives coverage. If the issue or the groups are unknown and undramatic, you may be better off going for one big splash.

When you publicize your issue, you are gaining recognition not only for the issue but for the group. That is critical. The more frequently your group's name appears in the news, the more likely that the public, and lawmakers in particular, will listen to what you say. When you get publicity on one issue, it means that on the next issue you will be listened to more carefully. Simply because your group's name appears regularly in the press, people will know that you are active.

When you do not get much press coverage for a while, people will believe you are losing your clout, no matter how hard you may be working. That is why it is so important to blow your own horn in the press. The press gives you the opportunity to tell the world how important the work you are doing is and how successful you have been. If you work on a problem with other groups, do not be shy about claiming your fair share of the credit.

Do not sit back and wait for spontaneous accolades to arrive. They will not.

Knowing that good press coverage can help make your group a force to be reckoned with, one of your main goals is to *develop a sufficient reputation so that you are considered a primary source of information and comment by the press.* Just as it is a sign of lobbying success when legislators start asking you for information, you have arrived when the press comes to you with questions.

It is in your interest to master a specific field, such as consumer protection — to be the first group the press turns to for comment. Reporters often call CCAG for comments on consumer, utility, environmental, and nuclear power stories. We even get regular requests from reporters for good questions to ask state officials at press conferences or on interview programs.

The first rule of good press coverage is that *everything you do is a news event.* Obviously, issuing a report or bringing charges is a news event, but so is every speech or testimony a staff member gives, every panel discussion in which you participate, every letter you write about local, state, or federal regulations, and every public statement you make as part of a coalition. Here are just some of the possibilities:

1. Issuing major statements or reports. Give out a press release summarizing your most important and persuasive points.

2. Testimony. Have a press release prepared every time you testify. A reporter's job is made a lot easier when you give him or her the highlights of your testimony in a one- or two-page release rather than in ten pages of testimony. You might issue a release about your testimony ahead of time, giving you double coverage—before the hearing and at the hearing.

3. Reactions to stories. Your reaction to a breaking news story is news. The story may be a court decision blocking a new superhighway from going through a park or a decision by the governor to support your position on a consumer-protection bill. You can also react publicly to a breaking national story that has state or local implications. When the United States Supreme Court declared that the setting of minimum fees by local bar associations was illegal, we immediately issued a release pointing out our work on the problem in Connecticut and warning that we would take the local bar association to court if it dragged its feet in complying with the decision. The story got us coverage across the state and an invitation to discuss the decision with the president of the Hartford Bar Association on a local television talk show. ·

The key is quick reaction time. Normally you have to react while the story is hot—the same day or, at the latest, the next day. You do not always have to issue a press release. Simply call up the local papers or wire services, ask if they are doing a story on the event, and say that you would like to comment.

4. Comments on state and federal regulations. Many individuals and groups comment on regulations proposed by state and federal agencies without any thought of attracting publicity to their comments. Why not release your comments to the press? We recently attracted much attention when we released comments we had made on regulations proposed by the U.S. Department of Housing and Urban Development that made only a feeble effort to remove poisonous lead paint from federal housing.

5. Speeches. You may be invited to speak to local groups— churches, fraternal organizations, women's groups—on your work. You should always have a press release ready for the speech. You are not going to get front-page coverage, but weekly papers or local reporters for dailies will often carry details of your speech if you let them know in advance that you will be speaking. Even if the reporter cannot attend, giving him or her your release means that you have a good shot at getting coverage. Local reporters are often hungry for stories.

Two points should be obvious by now. First, the possibilities for press coverage are limited only by your imagination. Second, always have a press release on hand, whether you are issuing a 50-page report, testifying before a legislative committee, or talking to the Timbucktoo Kiwanis Club. Remember, *you will normally get considerably more coverage if you give the press the major points of your study, testimony, or speech in a form and length that the press can most easily use.*

"Hard news" stories are not the only type of press coverage.

There are others that are sometimes even better at getting your message across. They include:

1. "Feature" stories in print or on television. Usually features are handled by people other than the regular news staff. This type of story is best suited to a description of some unusual aspect of your group—an interesting personality, how the group functions, or a special activity in which the group is participating. If you think you have a good subject for a feature story, let the appropriate news person know.

2. Letters to the editor (or responses to an editorial on radio or television). More people read the letters to the editor column than read the editorials. Letters can therefore be an extremely effective way to reach the community. For example, a letter to the editor is an excellent method for calling a legislator on the carpet for a vote that you believe was contrary to the public interest, especially where the vote is not likely to attract much attention elsewhere.

Encourage friends or supporters to do much of the letter writing, since it is effective to have the comments come from someone outside your group. Letters to the editor provide a good forum for prominent citizens who support your position to publicly express that support.

The best way to break into the letters column is to cite a recent editorial or news item related to your subject. If a legislator has commented publicly on your subject, you are ready to go. If not, try the indirect approach. For example, if a legislator who favors capital punishment announces opposition to abortion on the grounds that society is sanctioning the taking of human life, you could point out the irony of his or her strong support for the death penalty. Inconsistencies always have news value.

One cautionary note. Do not try to flood the paper with too many letters on one issue. Papers do not like to publish letters that look like part of an organized letter-writing campaign.

Finally, if you hear a radio or television editorial on which you would like to comment, do so. Radio and television stations are required to present differing points of view, and if yours differs from theirs, let them know about it. This is a marvelous way to get one or two minutes of careful public explanation of your position without any interruption or editing by a reporter or news editor. You do not have to disagree with the station's editorial. If you have a slightly different perspective or if you believe that the editorial did not go far enough, speak up. Once a local television station took what it believed was a strong stand in favor of mass transportation by recommending that at least 1 percent of all transportation funds be used for mass transit. We felt that the percentage should be closer to 20 and said so to the station, which soon had us on the air giving an editorial reply.

3. Editorial endorsements. The editorial support of your town's newspaper can carry tremendous weight. You should begin early to seek such support with a courteous visit to the editor to present your case. You should even explore the possibilities for an editorial cartoon.

Editorial support from prestigious papers can have two positive effects beyond boosting your issue. First, it can blunt the attack of anyone labeling you or your issue as "radical," "absurd," or "not to be taken seriously." If the *Timbucktoo Times* thinks your proposal is a good one or that your actions are "constructive," it is harder for other elements in the community to attack you as irresponsible without somehow implying that the *Times* is also wrong. Second, the support of the local paper will help with fundraising, especially from those who want evidence that the group they are contributing to is taken seriously by "responsible" segments of the community.

4. Weekly columns. How many times have you read a newspaper column and said, "I could write better than that"? Well, you can have the opportunity to do just that. While it is somewhat difficult to break into a daily paper, weekly papers, especially the local "shopper" papers, can be fertile ground for a column by your group. Even daily papers may be willing to run a well-written "guest column" occasionally. Many more people read these columns than you might imagine.

5. *Call-in shows.* Many radio stations have "talk lines," where listeners may call in and discuss almost anything not banned by the Supreme Court. Lining up people to call in their views on your issue can do much to broaden public awareness.

6. *Guest shows.* Guest shows and panel shows on local radio and television stations are also important vehicles for reaching the large numbers of people who regularly watch such programs. It is difficult to arrange a booking on one of these shows. Obviously, the more you and your issues are publicized, the more likely your request will be granted. You can help by making sure that the people who select interviewees or panelists know who you represent and the importance of what you and your group are doing.

If you are on a news interview show, it is always good to make at least one point that you have not made previously. If you have something newsworthy—a new campaign you are about to launch, information about or criticism of a state program—they will be much more likely to ask you back. Everybody likes fresh news.

These shows can even (although rarely) help bring in money. On "Face the State," a local television version of "Face the Nation," CCAG's director was asked about finances. He said that we needed money desperately and that if we did not get it, several major programs might have to be sacrificed. "What should we do?" he mused on camera. "Cut off the thirty-dollars-a-week salary of the person working on the problem of hazardous toys? Or should we let go our staff attorney, who earns five thousand dollars a year and who is the only person standing between the utility companies and higher rates for all customers?" In the ten days following this statement we received more than $7,000 in $2, $5, and $10 contributions, almost all from people who had never before contributed to the group.

7. Public service announcements, community billboards, and so forth. All radio and television stations are required by the Federal Communications Commission to air a certain number of hours per week of public service announcements (PSA's). This is free time, but it can only be used for information, such as educational material (warnings about unsafe toys, for example) or announcements of events, meetings, and the like. It cannot be used for propaganda, to denounce a legislator, push legislation, or otherwise express an opinion.

Call your local television and radio stations to find out their procedures for accepting PSA's. Some will ask for 10-second PSA's, some for 20 seconds; some prefer to get tapes; others will accept only a written script; some need the PSA one week before it is to be played; some ask for as much as three weeks' lead time.

YOUR AUDIENCE: THE PUBLIC

Your press work should be aimed at the general public. You are not writing for those who are already converts or who know the issue well. *Assume that your audience is unfamiliar with the issue.*

That may be hard to swallow. "How could the public not know about the issue?" you ask. Remind yourself that your top priority may not be the number-one item on the mind of every other citizen.

Do not go over the heads of your audience. Watch for catchwords or jargon that only people already familiar with the issue will understand ("trunklines," "capacity factors"). *Do not take knowledge of issues for granted.* Many people have no idea what a "generic" drug is.

It is often helpful to ask someone who is unfamiliar with the issue to read your release to see if that person understands it.

There may be times when you are aiming your comments not at the public at large but at a particular audience—a legislator, a group of legislators, your opposition, or your supporters. In a recent legislative session, a legislative leader said he was going to do something about the fuel-cost adjustment—an automatic pass-through to consumers of alleged higher fuel prices. At the same time, he did not seem to be listening to our objections to another fuel adjustment clause that would allow the utilities to pass on automatically the costs of nuclear plant shutdowns. That seemed inconsistent to us, so we called a reporter on one of the papers in the legislator's home city and told him about it. The next day our story appeared in the paper. A few days later the legislator stopped our director in the capitol and said, "I saw that article in the paper. Just what exactly is it that you want me to do?"

THE NEEDS OF THE PRESS

To use the news media effectively, you must understand and satisfy their needs.

1. Your story must be news. It should be as *action-oriented* as possible. Something must *happen*—something that will interest the public: a disclosure of secret information; scandal; dramatic damage to the public morality or health. This is what a reporter means when he or she tells you that the story must be "newsworthy." Motherhood and apple pie may be American favorites, but they are not newsworthy unless the mother has quintuplets, or the apple pie is 20 feet in diameter.

We recently participated in a hearing on the format for required posters listing the prices of prescription drugs. We prepared our sign and what we thought were tough suggestions to ensure that the sign would be readily seen by pharmacy customers. We fully expected our old antagonists, the pharmacists, to scream, yell, and generally carry on about how this sign was the worst poster in the world and would drive half the pharmacists in the state out of business. We carefully alerted a local consumer reporter to the anticipated clash. The morning of the hearings, the reporter walked in with film crew in tow, clearly excited at the prospect of a battle between CCAG and the State Pharmaceutical Association. We and he were equally surprised when the pharmacists endorsed all of our proposals. We had another surprise when we saw the reporter tell the camera crew, "Let's go. There's obviously no story here." (The reporter was wrong. For a consumer group and trade association to agree is far more unusual—and thus far more newsworthy—than for them to clash. Television news, however, thrives on visible conflict—pickets, shouting matches, and the like. Harmonious discussion makes poor footage.)

2. If you want television coverage, you must make your story *visual.* This is a vital point, but it is one that presents problems even for the most experienced group. For details, see the section on news conferences, later in this chapter.

3. Your story should include a positive *call for action.* We dislike, and we think the press and the public dislike, an approach that consists always and only of attacking without ever advancing some positive action. In every story, we attempt to suggest some remedy for the problem we are pointing out. There are times, of course, when you just have to challenge without proposing any solutions.

4. Your information must be *timely.* Timing is an important element of getting good press coverage. Your story should develop during or right after the controversy. Reporters will be much more interested in your reactions to the defeat or passage of a bill on the day it happens than they will three days later. The story is stale by then. Prepare statements ahead of time when you expect action on a bill in which you are

interested. The person or group who gets to the press first usually gets the story.

In addition to being aware of the timeliness of the story itself, you also need to be concerned with the particular time problems the press faces. The various media have different needs. Reporters for afternoon papers may need material by 8:30 a.m. to make the first edition. Television people often need their information by three in the afternoon for the evening news. Learn the deadlines for papers and broadcasts, and consider these deadlines when you release a story.

News releases should be sent to newspapers and radio and television stations ahead of time to give editors a chance to plan their coverage. Clearly mark the day, date, and hour you want your story released: FOR RELEASE 10 AM, WEDNESDAY, MAY 6, 1983.

We once got two calls from irate radio reporters because, through a wire service error, they thought we had put out a story for 6:30 p.m. release. One radio station broadcast local news on the half hour and on the hour, while our two angry friends only broadcast on the hour. Thus a 6:30 release would have given the other station a half-hour advantage. This may not seem important to you, but it certainly was important to the reporters.

Some specific points to remember:

• Releases are usually marked a.m. (giving afternoon papers first crack) or p.m. (giving morning papers the scoop).

• Try to divide releases evenly between a.m. and p.m. to avoid offending either group of newspapers.

• Releases marked for a.m. papers are generally used by the broadcast media the night before.

• Very little news happens on weekends and holidays. Releasing a story then is a good way to ensure more coverage. Monday morning papers in particular are usually starved for news. (Saturday papers usually report Friday's late news, and Sunday papers fill their space with features and lengthy review or analysis stories.) On the other hand, newsrooms—especially in radio and television—are understaffed on Sundays, often

run by one person, so do not hold press conferences on Sundays.
Nobody will come.

• You can also take advantage of seasonal lulls—during
the summer or around Christmas and New Year's Day. Of
course the audience can be as sparse as the news.

• Wednesday papers usually carry a great deal of
advertising—mainly supermarket ads. More ads mean more
pages and usually (not always) more space for news.

5. Do not assume special knowledge on the part of the
press. While members of the press may be able to grasp your
issues and arguments better than the general public, they are
seldom experts on all the issues they cover. They are deluged
with information, releases, and reports, and they have little
time to digest them. This seems to be especially true for
members of the broadcast media. In most cases you will have
more knowledge of the subject than the reporter you are
dealing with. You will have to explain carefully the importance
of your story. A reporter must interest the audience. You must
interest the reporter.

Any person who has worked with the press can cite examples
of misunderstandings or distortions of information, but such
a breakdown of communication usually reflects on the informant
as well as on the reporter. Misunderstandings may occur
because you did not explain the story carefully enough and
did not attempt to answer all questions. Treat reporters as if
they were new potential citizen lobby members—be enthusiastic
and understandable.

6. Remember that reporters have feelings. Like most other
professionals, members of the press can be very touchy when
they believe someone is trying to tell them how to do their job.
Another quick way to antagonize a press person (and thus to
hurt your cause) is to favor, or appear to favor, his or her
competitors. Reporters don't always need you, but you need
them. Another way to ruin a good working relationship is to
whine and complain about a given story and to demand that it

be rewritten your way the next day. (There are more effective ways to complain, and we will discuss those shortly.)

One CCAG staff member read a column discussing a legislator's vote on a key transportation issue and felt that the reporter had left out vital information. She called the columnist, pointed out the critical omission, and strongly suggested that the reporter correct it in his column the next day. The columnist made no response, but a short time later a friend of his told us that he had been "terribly offended." The omission was not corrected in the next day's paper and the reporter has ignored our releases religiously since that time, although he has printed attacks on our positions.

Writing Press Releases

Your releases should be written in clear, concise news style. *Write the release as you would like to see it appear in the paper.* Read the paper closely and write your ideal story so it sounds like one of the articles you have just read. That means you or your group should be referred to in the third person—"Good Guys, Inc., claimed today . . ." Avoid editorializing; instead, to express an opinion, use direct quotations and identify the sources of all quotations.

Use short words, short sentences, and short paragraphs. Your audience may not know that the issue *is* an issue, much less understand any esoteric arguments to support your position. Your statements should be quotable, the prose fresh, strong, and vivid. That does not mean that you should go overboard and accuse your opponent of wanting to destroy the health and safety of little children.

The lead—the first paragraph—is the most important paragraph of the release. It should make the major point of the story clearly and directly. The remainder of the release should follow what journalists call the "inverted pyramid" style: the most vital information at the beginning of the release, with subsequent paragraphs arranged in order of declining importance. This allows editors to cut the story from the bottom and leave the most important information.

Do not assume that the press or the public is familiar with your group. At an appropriate place in the release, often the last paragraph, there should be a brief description of the group.

If your group has a letterhead, use it. If not, head the release with the group's name, address, and telephone number. In addition, the name of a specific person who can answer questions should be at the top of the release. The release should have a headline, just like a newspaper story. If the release is more than one page long, write "MORE" at the end of each page except the last. Type "-30-" under the final paragraph to signify the end of the release.

The News Conference

News conferences are particularly important for radio and television. They serve several purposes. They can be good vehicles for initiating a major project: We have used them to launch our legislative profiles, our traveling center for auto complaints, and our intervention in a public utility rate case.

News conferences can also serve as the climax to an important story, preferably one with which your group has been identified in the news. Examples might be a victory in your fight to gain access to certain government materials, or your final resort to a lawsuit after all other means to bring about the recall of a defective auto have failed.

Finally, a news conference can be used to announce conclusions of a study (for example, the results of a consumer survey), or to expose injustices, or to call for a ban on plastic piping that is a fire hazard.

However, news conferences should be few and far between, limited to very important statements or events (as opposed to what might be a steady stream of releases from you). *The quickest way to diminish your overall press coverage, especially with radio and television reporters, is to call them to the well too many times.* They cannot put you on television every week, so do not ask them to, even if you think that what you have to say is important and deserves some visual coverage. If you call news conferences too often (more than one a month or so), you might be holding them with nobody there. Not only will that hurt your coverage, it will also depress the members of your group.

The key to a successful conference is careful planning. Your most important decision may be the format of the conference. The unfortunate fact is that form is often as important as content in communicating to the public. The traditional news conference with "talking heads" (people seated in discussion) is not as appealing as an event with action. You may find it fascinating to watch a panel of experts talk about your issue, but many people find this boring to watch, even for 30 seconds on the 6 o'clock news.

Innovation is the key. Your news conferences should lend themselves to exciting viewing. In planning your conference, do not be afraid to confer with television news directors, especially the friendly ones. Ask for advice without asking them for guaranteed coverage, which they would resent. You can say, "We're planning to release some very important information on a major tax dodge by a big corporation. We'd appreciate your keeping this under your hat for now, but we want to make the news conference worthwhile for you if you decide to cover it."

Here are a few specific things to keep in mind when planning a news conference:

1. Prepare the conference thoroughly, ahead of time. Rehearse it. If you are planning to ignite a piece of flammable sleepwear to illustrate the need for flame-retardant clothes, practice burning the garment at least once beforehand. We once held an outdoor conference where we tried to light a piece of plastic pipe. We did not count on the breeze; it took an embarrassingly long time to get the pipe burning.

2. The day before your conference, issue an "editor's advisory" over the wire services (Associated Press and United

Press International) announcing the time and place of the conference and the general topic. Keep the advisory short. In a sentence or two, tell why the conference is important and what visual events will take place. (Mentioning visuals is especially important to attract television cameras.) Include a telephone number and the name of a person to call for additional information. Do not spill the beans by giving away the main news of the conference. Whet the press's appetite: "An important press conference will be held describing a major state investigation that CCAG is launching." Giving out the hard news means that you may end scooping yourself and reducing the number of people at the news conference. To issue the advisory, call your local AP and UPI offices and say that you have an item to be listed in the "day book."

3. Call radio and television stations to tell them again early on the morning of the conference. Talk with the assignment editor or news director. Again, give the pertinent data and do a brief selling job for the conference.

4. Send local newspapers an advisory several days before the conference, and call them again the day before the conference. If there is a particularly good visual event at the conference, point that out so a photographer can be sent.

5. Make the location for the conference as easily accessible as possible. A television crew is much more willing to travel a mile from the studio than to traipse fifty miles into the hinterland. If the location is out of the way, be sure to include directions with your editor's advisory or phone calls.

6. If the location is outdoors, you must have an alternative indoor site in case of bad weather. Your decision to move the conference should be made in time to give the press adequate notice.

7. Begin the news conference with your statement and then open the floor for questions.

8. Deliver copies of any materials to be distributed at the

conference to the wire services a few hours ahead of time. The material should be embargoed (held for release) until the start of the news conference. Local wire service bureaus usually do not cover news conferences themselves because of insufficient staff. Most radio stations and many local newspapers get their news from the wire services so be sure that the wire services receive all materials released.

9. Have your release ready to hand out at the conference. The lead for the release should be the major point of your conference, not the fact that you are holding a news conference. For example, for a news conference on toy safety, the lead should be the need for more vigorous action to protect children from hazardous toys, not that you had a press conference where several unsafe toys were displayed. That point should be worked into the story, but it should not be the lead paragraph. Write the release as if the press conference had already taken place: "At a news conference today, CCAG Director Marc Caplan called for the banning of twelve ultrahazardous toys that are being sold in local stores."

Radio

Once you start getting press coverage, radio stations will call you for statements. This is fine, but you can also take the bull by the horns and call radio stations yourself to increase your coverage. Here are some instructions for handling radio audios:

1. Mail your releases to the stations you would like to cover the story.

2. Prepare a *one-minute* digest of the press release. Make it dynamic and include the highlights of the release. Practice doing it extemporaneously, since you should not read for audios (it sounds stiff). Eliminate "uhs" and "ums." Also be prepared with a 20-second summary you can slip into the conversation in case you don't get a chance for a longer statement. Have an outline of important points before you.

3. Be prepared to answer typical questions, such as "What is the significance of this survey?" or "What does your group want public officials to do?"

4. Call radio stations early on the morning of your release day. Also, find out which stations can be given audios a day ahead of time to run on the release day.

5. Avoid calling stations on the hour or half-hour since they are often doing live news shows then.

6. Ask for the newsroom, identify yourself and your group, and say you have a story they might be interested in. If no one is available in the newsroom, leave a message, but call back after 45 minutes. The newsperson will either let you elaborate on the story before expressing interest, or will want to put you on tape immediately. Be prepared for either, so you do not fumble between being conversational and doing a "dynamic" audio.

7. Indifference is sometimes shown by not calling you back. Take the hint if you have talked to a busy newsperson who says your call will be returned. But if a secretary takes the message, and the call is not returned, remember that the station is hectic and messages are easily lost. Try one more time.

8. Get names of newspeople who are particularly friendly to you; you stand a much better chance of getting on the air. Even if there is no particularly sympathetic reporter, it is easier and quicker to get through if you can simply say "Bob Jones, please" when you call, instead of explaining at length to whomever answers the telephone each time you call.

9. Radio newspeople are generally friendly or indifferent. Sometimes they ask good questions, rarely do they put you on the spot—they do not have enough time. Interview shows, obviously, are different.

10. When the station is taping, the phone will sound as if it is dead except for the "beep" some stations use when recording.

11. When the newsperson is ready to do an audio, either you will be asked to give your statement and follow up questions will then be asked, or the newsperson will begin by asking questions. If the questions are off the essential point, steer your answer toward what you want to say. Remember that the newsperson is trying to assimilate unfamiliar information and still have an interesting story. It is your job to respond to the questions and move into what you want to say. If you do not know the answer to a question and cannot give an estimate or a generalization you know to be true, do not fake it. Just say you do not know, and offer to check it out and call back (if appropriate).

12. Your statements should be colorful, and your voice should not be a monotone. Use inflection; stress important facts and figures. Be careful not to ramble. Think beforehand about what you will say, so that you can fit all the important points into a short statement. You will rarely get more than 30 seconds, so make it short and to the point. Do not be afraid to pause—they can just edit that out. If you make a factual error, tell the interviewer; it is easy to retape and much better than putting a mistake on the air. If you stumble over your words, keep on going. If it is bad it will be edited, but normal fluffs do not sound bad on radio.

13. Finally, if the interviewer leads into a question by summarizing your release and says something quite inaccurate, do not hesitate to break in and make a courteous correction. The intereviewer will appreciate your keeping the error off the air. Remember that most interviewers are trying to cooperate with you to produce a good story.

Basics for Better Coverage

To maximize your coverage, remember these basics:

1. A standard press list is a must. For a statewide group it should include all the newspapers in the state, both dailies

and weeklies. You should have the name of the editor or news director for each, along with other contacts, such as particularly friendly reporters or people who might have a special interest in your story (local reporters if the story has a local flavor, environmental reporters if the story deals with air pollution). You may also want to include editorial writers on the list. Make up address labels and photocopy them to save the time of typing envelopes each time you do a release.

2. Do not forget small newspapers. These papers will often give you excellent coverage. Several weeklies in Connecticut often run our releases as their main story.

3. Be sure to give the wire services copies of all your releases. Most news outlets—broadcast and print—use one or both wire services. Some papers will not use your release but will run the wire service story on your release. (The opposite can also be true. Many papers dislike giving a wire service byline to a local story.) The best way to cover yourself is to see that everyone, including the wire services, gets your releases.

4. Deliver releases by hand to local news outlets. We have found that when the release is dropped off in person, we receive better coverage than when we rely on mail delivery. Maybe it is simply psychological, but handing the release to a reporter or a news editor gives your story more impact. It is almost like saying, "This release is important enough that I'm handing it to you." Dropping off a release gives you the opportunity to talk to an editor or reporter and explain the importance of your story. Hand delivery is also faster than mail delivery. Of course it takes more of your work and time, but by now you realize that, as in other parts of your legislative effort, success comes only with those two ingredients. Sometimes you should forgo a statewide mailing of your release. You may be responding to fast-breaking developments in the capital, and if the release is mailed, the story will be old (and therefore of very little news value) when the media get it. Under those circumstances, we do only a local press run. We hand-deliver releases to all

capital-area media, to reporters assigned to the capitol, and to the wire services (the key to getting your statement out across the state immediately).

5. If you think your story might have national appeal, be sure to include key people from the national media— *Time, The Wall Street Journal, The Washington Post, The New York Times, The Los Angeles Times, The Chicago Sun Times,* National Public Radio, and so forth. Also include specialized publications if your story is in their area of interest—for example, *Business Week, The American Banker.*

6. Releases and announcements of news conferences should usually be sent to city editors or assignment editors. The editor—not the reporter—determines what gets covered and what kind of play it gets. That does not mean that you should not prime particular reporters to whom you have talked about the story previously or who you know would be interested in the story. These reporters, as well as the news or assignment editor, should get the release.

7. When you have a particularly important story, prepare the media for it in advance. When we released our study of the members of the Connecticut legislature and our profiles on all Republican and Democratic candidates for governor, we not only called every newspaper and radio and television station, but also went around the state before publication, visiting every news editor to discuss the importance of the project. In some cases this encouraged preliminary stories on the legislative study, building public anticipation of the actual release of the project.

8. Whenever you put out a report longer than a few pages (or longer than ten minutes' reading) always issue a brief summary too. The reporters' time, interest, or familiarity with the issue may be limited. Giving them a summary ensures that they will at least get the highlights of the report. Having a summary, of course, does not mean that you forget about

writing a release. As we emphasized previously, you should issue a release any time you want press coverage.

9. Space your releases for maximum effect. A whistleblower in a state government has just given you a series of memoranda from the state's consumer protection commissioner disclosing that in five separate instances the department changed regulations because of interference from the governor's office. Do you release it in one flurry, getting a single big story? Or do you release a different memorandum once a week or every other week, getting even more publicity each time, building anticipation for the next story? The answer seems obvious.

By spacing a story over a period to time, you can keep the issue (and you) in the news for a longer time. Of course, spacing may give you a series of small stories and nothing more. You have to play it by ear.

10. Joint or coalition releases are another way to maximize coverage of your issue. Have other groups endorse your position either one at a time or simultaneously. This can be especially effective when the combination of organizations is unusual — for example, a chemical manufacturer and an environmental group taking a united position on hazardous waste legislation.

Discretion is advisable here. You will not want to be associated with every organization in the state. Choose your partners carefully.

11. Your reputation with the press and the public depends on your credibility. Be accurate. Tell the truth. You want the press to have confidence in what you are saying. If you do not know the answer to a question, say so.

Be careful when using information supplied by another group. If possible, verify it yourself before going public with it. At the very least, acknowledge in your statements the source of the information. Use such phrases as: "According to . . ." or "Using figures supplied by . . ."

Personal Relations with the Press

When and how do you complain? Common sense should guide your relations with press people. Approach them as you approach your colleagues or members of the legislature.

If you think the coverage you have gotten (or have not gotten) is unfair, approach the problem carefully. Do not start out by going over the reporter's head, yelling at his or her boss, or threatening to file a complaint with the Federal Communications Commission because a television newscaster raised his or her eyebrows while doing a story on you. First make sure you have a legitimate complaint. What did other papers or stations do on the same story? Has this happened several times before?

If you feel there is a serious problem, by all means let your feelings be known. Talk to the reporter first. Your approach should be honest, but gentle. Rather than accuse the reporter of deliberately misstating your position or ignoring your story, you might take the approach of asking for advice: "How should we be presenting our stories?" "How can we improve our coverage?" "What kinds of things would you be interested in from us?"

That is the first approach. If your coverage does not improve, you need to go to the news editor and again try the gentle approach. Your tone should become increasingly firm if problems occur and your hints are not working.

At all times, you should simply point out why the coverage was unfair. It is unwise to make threats — either with legislators or with the press. Your yelling and threatening will only further harm your coverage.

CCAG's coverage has generally been very good, but we have spoken to reporters when we think they have missed important elements of a story. Our tone is always one of providing more information, not demanding that a new story be written. On occasion, when we have complained about our coverage, the news editor has invited us to write an op-ed article.

Do you like compliments for the work you have done? So do reporters. When you see a good story or editorial, tell them so.

We have found that, perhaps not surprisingly, we get our best coverage from reporters who know us and who appear to be comfortable in working with us. You do not have to be a back slapper, but nurturing relations and friendships with members of the press pays dividends. Most reporters are nice folks and enjoyable to be and work with. We have lunch on occasion with some friendly reporters. At the capitol we carry on joking conversations with the capitol press corps and try to get to know as many as possible on a first-name basis. That means, of course, spending a considerable amount of time at the capitol but—as you have already heard many, many times in this book—if you want to be successful, you simply have to put in the time. New staff members often asked CCAG's director how we got such good coverage on matters on which we had not even issued a press release. His response was simply: "I was around the capitol and a reporter—who considers me a friend—wanted a comment."

SUMMARY

1. The press can make or break an issue.

2. Try to become a primary source of information and comment for the press.

3. Everything you do is a news event, from issuing a 100-page report to giving a speech at a local garden club.

4. Underutilized press possibilities include feature stories, letters to the editor, editorial endorsements, weekly columns, call-in and guest shows, and public service announcements. Do not ignore them.

5. Aim your press work at the general public and at the press itself.

6. Always assume that neither the public nor the press knows anything about your issue.

7. *Be aware of the needs of the media: action, visual components, and timeliness.*

8. *Remember that press people have feelings too.*

9. *Write your releases clearly and concisely.*

10. *Plan your news conferences carefully.*

11. *Remember the mechanics: who to give what, when to give who what, and how to give who what and when.*

12 *Spacing a series of releases over an extended period can be extremely effective.*

13. *Above all, be accurate.*

☆ **6** ☆
Fundraising

You are in the middle of a big legislative battle. You must get a mailing out to 2,500 supporters to generate constituent pressure vital to your bill's passage. You also want to bring several busloads of people to the capitol to demonstrate public support for the bill at a hearing. Without either, the bill is lost.

The post office wants $175 for postage, and the printer wants $120 for the flyers. The bus company wants $400 for the bus rentals. You cannot afford any of them.

The constant need to raise money haunts most citizen groups. Many advocates feel that it is crass to devote a lot of time, energy, or thought to raising money, but is is essential for a successful lobbying effort. Money is needed to win. We are not talking about funds for throwing lavish parties, wining and dining legislators, or for a plush, carpeted office. Money is needed for mailings, stamps, printing, mimeographing, traveling, and telephone calls. These are expenses you will face even if you do not have an office or a full-time staff. If you want to hire staff or rent an office, you will need more money.

There are some very low-budget groups operating out of someone's living room that have managed to be very influential at the state legislature. Those organizations are indeed remarkable and are probably models of financial efficiency. Decent funding, however, while not the most vital ingredient for a successful lobbying effort, is very important.

The time to think about the dollars you will need is not in the middle of a legislative fight when you are about to send out an emergency mailing and rent three buses for a rally at the capitol. The time is long before that.

It does not take a crystal ball to help you plan the costs of a legislative campaign. You need something much more mundane, but much more useful. You need a budget.

DETERMINING HOW MUCH YOU NEED

A budget is simply a projection of expenses and receipts. Budgeting is a way of translating your goals and plans into dollars and cents to see if you have enough dollars and cents to accomplish your goals and plans.

Budgeting requires a series of educated guesses. The more educated the guesses, the more valuable the budget. You begin with an examination of what specific goals you hope to achieve during the budget period (six months, say, or one year). Next, list everything you expect to do to achieve those goals. How many mailings will you need and at what cost; how many bus rentals will be required; how much must be spent on the phone at the going rate? Your estimates may range from pure guesses to exact amounts, but they will help you determine how much money you will need and how you are going to raise it.

The budget forces you to list the things that you want to do, assigns a cost to each, and allows you to make informed decisions about which actions will most efficiently serve your goals, and which are expendable. The budget tells you what you need. Now you have to figure out how to get it.

HOW TO BEGIN RAISING WHAT YOU NEED

Americans give away a lot of money. In one recent year they contributed more than $24 billion to charities. That exceeds the assets of Coca-Cola, Xerox, General Foods, Firestone, Lockheed, Bethlehem Steel, U.S. Steel, and RCA combined.

There is money out there to be raised but, as you may have guessed, it is not an easy task. Budgeting helps you plan, and planning helps you organize your fundraising so that it is cost and time-effective. *The most important goal of your fundraising should be to make the most money using the least amount of your and your supporters' time.* In other words, your fundraising efforts should emphasize efficiency.

We emphasize efficiency because we found that we had been taking too much of our staff and supporters' time on fundraising with minimal results. Efficiency is calculated by estimating the amount of money you reasonably expect to raise from a project and dividing by the number of hours of work required for the project.

It is not that cut and dried, of course. Many fundraising projects have worthwhile side benefits that cannot be precisely computed, such as increased public exposure, membership recruitment, and leadership development. But remember that you should not spend all your time fundraising and probably do not want to. Your purpose is to pass important legislation and to build an effective citizen organization.

FINDING SOMEONE TO DO IT

We have found that the best way to maximize the efficiency of a fundraising program is to have one person—whether staff member or volunteer—responsible for fundraising. We lost large amounts of our time in the past on fundraising. The staff took precious time away from their lobbying, which they are quite skilled at, to struggle with raising money, which they are not. The result was often slackened efforts to pass legislation, poor fundraising results, and frustrated staff.

Having one person in charge does not mean that staff members or volunteer lobbyists can wash their hands of the need to raise money. All members of your group need to understand your financial needs, the need to limit expenditures, and the importance of keeping a sharp eye out for fundraising possibilities in their work. They should also be prepared to help with fundraising when their time can be used efficiently.

Instead of drafting a member of the staff to coordinate fundraising, you may want to consider hiring professional fundraisers. Our history with professional fundraisers has been mixed. Like most professions, fundraising has its fools and geniuses, journeymen and experts, followers and innovators. Our only advice here is to be extremely cautious; nobody can perform miracles and anyone promising them should be viewed very suspiciously. *Completely* check out the background of any professional you plan to hire.

Your fundraiser has been chosen — staff, volunteer, or outside professional. Your budget has told you how much you need. Now you have to figure out how to raise it.

Many people have dabbled in elementary fundraising at one time or another — selling cookies door-to-door perhaps, or sponsoring a benefit car wash. Though such familiar fundraising techniques are useful, you probably need to consider more lucrative ways of raising money. There is no dearth of creative fundraising ideas. An entire book could be devoted to a brief explanation of merely half of them. We will simply note some of the ways we have raised money successfully since our beginnings in 1971.

For several years we raised money mainly through membership dues and various money-raising events such as movies, concerts, cycle-thons, coffee klatches, and paid speaking engagements.

CCAG's most successful fundraising venture, however, has been the door-to-door canvassing program we began in 1976. Canvassing is a traditional way of gathering information and soliciting support for electoral politics, community fund drives, and public opinion surveys. But it has taken on added significance recently as a means of financial support for grass-roots citizen organizations and public issue campaigns.

CCAG canvassers are full-time paid employees. They go door-to-door in different neighborhoods every weekday evening. Each canvasser is assigned a certain "territory," marked on a map, to cover. In a single night the average canvasser will walk three miles and knock on 70 doors. A professional canvassing operation is vastly different from gathering a few volunteers and sending them out to knock on doors.

Canvassers have two tasks. The first is, obviously, to raise money for the group. They generally ask for donations of anywhere from $3 to $10, and if someone shows unusual interest in the organization they might suggest a larger contribution.

Each canvasser has a quota — a minimum amount of money to be raised each night — so that the canvass maintains high efficiency.

Aside from fundraising, canvassing provides a very direct and personal communication and education function for the group. Canvassers have the opportunity to tell citizens individually about CCAG programs and issues, disseminate educational materials, encourage active participation, and get valuable feedback.

These two functions of canvassing, efficient fundraising and community outreach, have allowed CCAG to significantly expand its budget and program, including increasing its influence in the legislature.

One final note on canvassing: It is not as easy as it sounds. Canvassers must be carefully trained and closely supervised. Turnover is high. The job is tough. And it is not cheap. Start-up costs of a canvassing program are high. A sizeable portion of the money raised must be spent on running the program. For many small organizations, canvassing is simply not practical.

Foundation grants, though a popular source of income for some kinds of public interest groups, are difficult to get if you are a lobbying organization.

Full-time lobbying organizations, although tax *exempt,*

are not tax-*deductible* for contributors. As a result, foundations and big contributors will usually look elsewhere to give away their money. You can, however, establish an educational, tax-deductible "sister organization" to receive contributions. The League of Women Voters, among many others, has gone this route. Consult an attorney if you are considering it.

Do not hesitate to present a personal picture of the financial realities of your organization in your fundraising pitch. Low salaries, long working hours, and a spartan office are the kinds of things potential donors should be made aware of. It not only generates (perhaps well-deserved) sympathy and respect, but it also demonstrates that you use money carefully and are a truly committed bunch.

Diversify your funding. A wealthy philanthropist has taken a sudden interest in your group and offers you a whopping $50,000 grant. The money will almost totally fund your lobbying activities. You accept the grant. Unfortunately, this wealthy supporter has a personal penchant for consumer protection legislation, and an equally avid dislike for utility rate reform measures—one of your top priorities. You may successfully resist the pressure he will undoubtedly apply to change those priorities, but you will have to expend a lot of energy to do it. And next year, it is likely that there will be *no* money forthcoming from his coffers.

A basic goal of your fundraising program should be to make it self-sufficient. No single institution or entity outside your group should control a large portion of your budget. It is easy to become the victim of a single source of money.

Get good leadership. The most important component of any fundraising effort is leadership. A strong person running a relatively weak fundraising idea can turn it into a smashing success, but a weak leader can turn the best idea into a dismal failure.

We have learned this the hard way. We have had different

people handle the same type of fundraising effort. Some produced and others did not. The key is the person's track record. Check it carefully before you hire—or designate— your fundraiser. If you cannot find someone with experience, choose a fundraiser who is organized and personable with strong leadership qualities.

Don't be shy. Most people hate to ask other people for money face-to-face. Almost every fundraising devise was invented to ease the agony of asking for money.

Think about the number of ways you have been asked to give to good causes. There is the telephone, the door collection, the counter-top coin box, the raffle, the auction, the concert, the bake sale, and many, many others. Which one gets the most money from you? Face-to-face fundraising appeals are, as a rule, vastly more effective than those that insulate the fundraiser from the contributor. If you are like most people, you respond best when somebody looks you in the eye and asks.

We have had many coffee klatches and after-dinner receptions that generated tremendous enthusiasm but raised no money simply because no one at the event dared to speak up and say, "Will you please give us $15 or $25 right now."

If you work hard to get several hundred people to your event and do not ask them for contributions, you have missed a golden opportunity. How can you possibly recapture the feeling created by a great speaker when you talk to your prospect three days later? How can you see and talk to everybody who attended? Do you dare risk everything you have worked for in the hope that your guests will mail you a check? Only a few will, and they won't give as much as they would have at the event.

Publicity is a means, not an end. Publicity alone does not raise money. Never assume that simply getting publicity about your fundraising event or your activities will bring in money. Publicity will not bring in money; you will. Publicity can help you by creating a favorable climate for your efforts. If people have heard about you or know of the work you are doing, it makes them much more receptive when they are asked to give money. But *they must be asked.* Do not confuse general public awareness of your group with the need to do in-person fundraising.

Keep good records. Fundraising professionals have proven that the best people to ask for money are people who have *already* given you money. Clear, current records make this easy. *Never throw out the name of someone who has given you money or shown interest in your work.*

If you have more than several thousand names in your possible donor list, you may need a computer to keep track of the information. (Relax; you do not have to buy a computer. There are mailing houses that specialize in maintaining membership lists and preparing mailing labels, usually for a per-member fee.)

Keep contributors informed. Most contributors, if they are enthusiastic about your group, will become very interested in your activities. They want you to tell them why their contribution was a good investment. Keep your contributors up to date on your activities. Even a simple mimeographed one-page newsletter listing recent and upcoming events lets contributors know that their money is *doing* something, and it makes them more likely to contribute in the future. This regular flow of information to contributors also serves another function: It helps build your political base. Contributors can become your most active supporters, ready to work on issues that you have helped them become interested in.

Play by the rules. Before plunging ahead with your fundraising endeavors, you should check local and state laws to make sure you are complying with them. Being accused of violating fundraising laws not only subjects you to potential penalties but also provides the kind of publicity you don't want or need.

One final note. Many organizations unable to provide you with direct financial help can give you in-kind contributions. Churches and labor unions are especially helpful in this area. They can assist with mailings, paper, mimeographing, supplying meeting halls, or getting their members to help your group.

This fundraising chapter was intentionally brief. The following are just some of the recent books that cover the subject in detail, and should be must reading for anyone seriously interested in maintaining a citizen action group:

1. *The Grass Roots Fundraising Book* by Joan M. Flanigan
   The Youth Project
   1000 Wisconsin Avenue, N.W.
   Washington, DC 20007
2. *The Grantseeker's Guide: A Directory of Social Change Organizations* by Jill R. Shellow
   National Network of Grantmakers
   919 North Michigan Avenue, Fifth Floor
   Chicago, Illinois 60611
3. *Law and Taxation: A Guideline for Conservation and Other Non-Profit Organizations* by Berlin, Roisman, and Kessler
   The Conservation Foundation
   1717 Massachusetts Avenue, N.W.
   Washington, DC 20036

SUMMARY

1. Adequate financial resources are often necessary for a successful legislative campaign.

2. Develop a budget for each campaign.

3. Select efficient fundraising strategies.

4. *Your funding should come from diverse sources to insure financial stability and program independence.*

5. *Keep good financial records.*

6. *Keep contributors informed about your activities.*

7. *Choose a fundraising strategy that will produce the revenue you need.*

8. *Direct mail fundraising and canvassing are lucrative, but require substantial administrative resources.*

9. *Integrate public education about your issues into your fundraising efforts.*

10. *Fundraising is as important as any activity in which your group is engaged.*

☆ 7 ☆

Legislative Committees

A bill regulating debt collectors is being debated on the floor of the House. The debate is going well; the speakers appear concerned about protecting consumers. Suddenly an argument breaks out between committee chairpeople about which committee should have considered the bill—general law or banking. It is just a minor point, you think. What difference could it make now? The next thing you know, the challenging committee has won—the bill is sent back to a different committee, killing it for the year.

Surprised? If so, you have a lot to learn about the legislature's committee system.

THE COMMITTEE SYSTEM

Committees are the primary work units of the legislature. Legislatures, like other large organizations, use the committee system to divide up their work. A legislative body as a whole simply cannot consider every item that comes before it. More than 20,000 bills a year are introduced in some of the larger states.

Since the committees are where legislators spend much of their time, and since committee work precedes floor work, the committee is where legislators get to know one another and try to assert their own priorities. And that is where you should get to know them, the staff, other lobbyists, and the committee process. For CCAG lobbyists, the committee offices soon became second homes.

The key to your effectiveness in working with a committee is your credibility, which you must establish early. If you are part of an organization with an established reputation, identify yourself with that reputation from the outset. If you are starting from scratch, try to present yourself or your research in a way that will be helpful to the committee. In either case, present yourself as a person interested in the committee's work, willing and able to supply information.

The Rules Committee

Most state legislatures have one committee in each house that reigns supreme over all other committees—usually called the rules committee. Other committees have restrictions on their power; the rules committee writes those restrictions.

The rules committee usually has only a few members—the top leaders of the house—and, in some cases, is a committee in name only. In one state, it is common knowledge that the Senate rules committee never meets: The majority leader simply acts in the committee's name.

In many states, bills that have been reported out of committee must then go through the rules committee before reaching the floor. In theory, the rules committee simply acts as an expediter or manager, scheduling bills for action and keeping things flowing smoothly. In practice, the rules committee exercises total control over legislation in those states that follow this procedure.

The rules committee is usually the only committee that continues functioning after the deadline for reporting of bills: Any bills not acted on by committees at that point are referred to the rules committee, where they often remain.

Committee Mechanics

The areas of jurisdiction of standing committees usually

parallel those of executive agencies, allowing for legislative oversight and potentially clear and direct avenues of two-way communication between the branches of government.

Connecticut is the only state with all *joint* committees; that is, committees are made up of members from both houses, with co-chairpersons and ranking members drawn from each. In other states your efforts will be divided between House and Senate counterparts (except, of course, in Nebraska's one-house legislature).

In most states, hearings are open to the public, but executive or voting sessions may be closed. If committee meetings are closed to you, your first priority should be to open them up. (Join other groups, such as Common Cause, to do so.)

The Chairpeople

The frenetic nature of committees seems ready-made for one- or two-person rule, and such is often the case. Chairpeople have a magician's hatful of subtle and not-so-subtle tricks that they can produce to protect or destroy bills. This can work for you as well as against you. The chair of a committee considering several of our bills once suddenly adjourned a meeting, citing "another important commitment." Out in the hall he said, "Did you see who was there!" Troubled by the presence of an unexpected number of conservative and Republican members, he simply put off the key votes until more loyal troops could be called out.

One way for the chairperson to dominate the committee is to restrict the flow of information to members. In Connecticut, it was easy to see the contrast between the general law committee, where the staff spent hours collecting and distributing bills and information to members, and the judiciary committee, where only the chairperson was actually looking at the bill the committee was voting on.

Committee chairpeople should be your primary lobbying targets from the first day you walk into the capitol. They make powerful allies and formidable opponents.

Before the session begins, meet with the chairpersons of

the committees your bills are likely to go through. They are generally willing to meet.

If you have done your groundwork and know a chairperson's pet project or a special issue that the committee has to confront, you might offer him some tangible work he can use on the topic.

The purpose of your initial meeting is to get acquainted, to introduce your role, as you would like it to be understood, and to indicate your willingness to shape it to be compatible with the committee's work. Thus, "I'll be attending meetings. I'll be happy to prepare a memo on this for you," or "I have a summary of that for you. I'm meeting with the pharmacists (or any experts or opposition) now to develop this legislation," or "I hope you'll call on me to answer any questions . . . I'd like to work with your research staff . . ." are appropriate exit lines. Try to leave the chairperson with an expectation that you will produce something, and with the understanding that you are interested in the subjects the committee deals with, not just in getting your bill out of the committee.

The Members

Get to know the committee members. By diligently attending meetings, and coming early and staying as late as some of them do, you will gain respect from them and the staff. It is important that you be identified by all as a permanent fixture, or, as a CCAG lobbyist was once described, "an *ad hoc* member of the committee."

Introduce yourself, repeatedly if necessary. If your function relates only to a limited part of the committee's jurisdiction, identify your focus: "I'm working on the bottle bill," or "I'm interested in the Small Claims Court reform bill before your committee." Identify your particular expertise, if relevant: "I'm a public interest lawyer working on consumer credit issues"; "I'm a nuclear physicist." Consider wearing some identification, such as a button with your group's name. (Since 1978, lobbyists in the Connecticut capitol have been required to wear identification badges.) Sometimes it is hard to avoid being mistaken for legislative staff, but it can create resentment. You can also be less threatening without any identification, but you generally like to know who other people are, and they usually feel the same way.

Key your lobbying strategy to selected legislators. When seeking supporters, look not only for those you can convince, but for those respected enough to convince others. Legislators lobby each other and some legislators establish themselves as authorities, or find themselves so regarded, on particular issues for the committees on which they serve. One of the few attorneys on the general law committee was looked to for answers on all zoning questions, even though he rarely attended meetings. In the judiciary committee, with different specialities among the lawyer members, it was simply understood that the committee would not discuss bills in certain areas unless the resident expert was present.

The Staff

Meet the staff, especially the research staff. Try to get them to see you as an adjunct member, a colleague. Personal relations, as always, depend on a variety of factors, but some staff people will welcome you as co-workers—a relationship easily turned to your advantage by keeping them thoroughly informed about your bills and your positions so that they in turn share information with you. Clerical staff have access to valuable information such as bill status and votes. They also converse, and like to commiserate about the heat, the cold, the coffee, or a legislator. Sometimes they can provide you valuable insights.

Research staff deal with the substance of particulars addressed to the committee, technical matters that need attention, and questions that members want answered. The overlap between your work and theirs can easily be seen, and mutual cooperation makes sense. The staff, as the intermediary, will help determine the type of relationship you have with committee members.

The staff can control, as much as anyone can, the information that legislators routinely get, except on heavily lobbied issues. This applies to the amount of information, the type of information, the access to information, and very importantly, the judgments concerning it. Legislators do not have—or do not take—the time to read everything themselves. When a lot of unsolicited literature comes in, staff people select what seems important. Material distributed to legislators is often accompanied by staff comments: "Did you see this riduculous letter from that professional society?" or "That study was out of date five years ago."

The staff also control the information *you* get. You have probably already determined what is "public" information. You will also learn that what is "available" depends on you and your relationships. You may be able to add your name to a committee mailing list, and the staff may give you agendas or tell you what is in the wings. Ask staff members for copies of materials that are distributed to committee members.

Get copies of materials that other lobbyists give out or receive. Staff members can also pass along to you legislators' questions and comments. They can tell you about planned floor strategy or other lobbying activity that they have seen but you have not. If they prepare floor statements for legislators, they may share these with you, or seek your help in the preparation, as may legislators themselves. Staff members may give you advice.

Occasionally, staff may even do your job for you. A consumer protection bill once came up before an unreceptive committee while our lobbyist was at another meeting. A staff member (possibly won over by our steady barrage of memos) piped up with our arguments. Within five minutes the committee was convinced, and our lobbyist returned to find the day already won.

The Special Interests

Some committees may appear to be dominated by special interests with direct financial stakes in the committees' actions.

Lobbyists for banks or retail stores may be given a cordial welcome and a friendly ear while a consumer representative seems incapable of convincing the committee that the world is not flat. The direct access of special interest groups to the committee is sometimes assured by legislative conflicts of interests: for instance, the real estate committee may be loaded with real estate agents.

On occasion public policy may be decided by struggles between committees—each defending its own private interests. All too often the public interest does not coincide with any of the omnipresent special interests. Battling against conflicts of interest is in itself a worthy goal for any public interest lobbyist to pursue.

The Public Interest Lobbyist

Obviously, your personality, as much as your abilities, will shape the image you project. You should stress your role as a resource person, a provider of disinterested and thorough research. As you will be contending with professionals for the attention of people who are likely to be impressed by professionalism, your style should be professional as well. Eccentricities are probably best left at home. Think about whether you will cut your hair or wear business suits.

Do not throw your weight around; do not threaten. Public interest lobbyists should not play that game. Do-gooders tend to be proud, so you may dislike showing deference to some backslapping lawmaker who happens to control important votes. But remember that you may well find yourself asking for a legislator's support on issues that are unpopular (at least among legislators). A good relationship or reputation with legislators can be your biggest asset.

Expertise and Efficiency

We found that the expertise of committee members was closely linked to the prestige of the committee and its degree of specialization. The judiciary committee, composed almost exclusively of lawyers, was a gathering of experts; the general law committee, with a hundred areas of responsibility—zoning, special revenue, consumer protection, state holidays, consumer credit, occupational licensing—could not possibly be expert in all of them.

Difficulties in coping with a vast range of problems are inherent in any legislative body, especially a part-time one. But to our dismay, we quickly learned that some committees failed to make efficient use of the limited staff and other resources that were available to them. One committee chairperson was unaware that the legislative aide assigned to his committee was an attorney. The legislator's temperament —his frequent impatience—meant he often did not bother to look for or wait for someone with appropriate knowledge, giving short shrift to things he did not understand. And it was frustrating indeed to testify to empty tables at public hearings and later hear members asking simple questions that they would have had answered if they had bothered to read memos or attend their own hearings.

Some committees are simply careless—not bothering to eliminate incompatible bills, send misdirected ones to the proper committee, check into overlaps with other committees, or reconcile new legislation with laws already on the books. You may sometimes have to do a legislator's job by performing these tasks. Remember that legislators' lack of information provides a major opening for all lobbyists. Always look for opportunities to supply information, even at the last minute and even to the most indifferent legislators.

Too Much to Do, Too Little Time

Faced with yet another day when two committees on which she served had scheduled meetings for the same time, one new senator lamented that she could not divide herself in half to attend both. We once tried to round up committee votes on a crucial utility bill by asking members who had never made it to the meetings to show up, "just this once." One senator, the chair of another time-consuming committee, just laughed when we reminded him that he was also a member of the regulated activities committee.

Many representatives simply choose to devote most of their time to a favorite committee. While this may seem a practical approach, it tends to produce committees dominated by small groups with narrow-minded attitudes toward their subject areas—and often with conflicts of interest as well.

Legislators' inability or unwillingness to attend to their committee work creates a huge informational void that you (and special interest lobbyists) will try to fill. When legislators do not do their homework, do it for them and try to get them to rely on you for it.

The Cast in Performance

Although the formal procedures in the committee room may not tell the whole story, they provide an invaluable look at various people in action. You see who comes, who stays, who hobnobs, and who dislikes whom. You see who comes in without knowing what's going on and votes as someone tells them to. You get indications of who is conscientious or trustworthy. You see who speaks and how well, who asks questions and who answers.

You see who offers amendments and who consistently says "me too." You can watch for evidence of conflicts of interest. Some people cannot resist doing a little lobbying on their own behalf in what must feel like a less visible forum than floor debate. Some do so much damage here with their committee votes that a later abstention on the floor is pure charade. A little citizen watchdogging helps reduce this.

You also see other lobbyists. As always, be civil; you may be able to arrange to share work and information, to your mutual benefit.

Committee Meetings

Committees gather for several different purposes during the year. Their most frenzied moments occur during voting sessions as deadlines loom. But other types of committee sessions — some impromptu and some in strange surroundings — offer valuable opportunities that you should watch for.

Your ability to take part in the more formal proceedings of the committees will depend on the rules and customs of your legislature. During formal meetings, we generally found we could not speak unless asked a specific question. But your role as a committee "regular" sometimes may permit easier and more frequent participation.

Legislators' conferences are held very early in the committee process. There, lawmakers can speak formally to push or simply explain their own bills. State agencies are also invited to comment on proposed legislation and suggest new legislation.

These encounters may also serve to introduce agency personnel to the committee (and to you). You will probably just sit and listen, but you can discover which agencies support what, and then team up, when you can, with those that suit you.

We found that working sessions and seminars varied greatly from committee to committee, ranging from formal lectures or panel discussions to informal gatherings. Educational sessions tended to draw the more-interested members, permitting a more relaxed and thorough discussion of issues. The impetus for such optional sessions may come from the legislators or an influential staff member, from public pressure on hot issues, *or from you.* You may be able to participate in or even run these. Especially when they are informal, such meetings allow you to develop a better working relationship with legislators and to identify the recognized experts or resource people the committee turns to on particular subjects. These sessions are held infrequently. Make the most of them.

There is a thin line between a truly educational session and a carte-blanche day for some lobby. One chairperson curtly dismissed a slick pharmaceutical company lobbyist seeking to "educate" the committee with a public relations film, but a representative from the credit department of a very large retail chain was invited to give an extended explanation of credit intricacies. A member of a national study commission, brought in as an expert, had been treated quite brusquely moments before. Such disparate treatment of lobbyists underscores the importance of carefully cultivated good relations with committees and their chairpeople.

Subcommittee Meetings

You may find that portions of committee workloads are delegated to subcommittees. There is no set pattern: one committee in Connecticut had 22 subcommittees; others had none.

Subcommittees often operate less formally than committees, letting you play a greater role. The smaller number of legislators in the group also makes it easier to identify the real workers, those you can single out for efforts at close cooperation.

Subcommittees often accomplish more between sessions than during sessions. Often formulated in direct response to a failing of the previous session or a need made clear during it, interim subcommittees can consult experts, conduct hearings, and conduct studies before recommending legislation—all without the pressures always present during the session.

Subcommittee service tends to increase legislators' commitment to an issue. Once they have worked closely on an issue and know it thoroughly, legislators are more likely to push for legislation.

In the Nooks and Crannies

Keep in mind that formal meetings are only the visible portion of a committee's work—the tip of the iceberg.

In addition to these scheduled meetings of committees and subcommittees, there are other gatherings, some of which you may be able to attend. It can be vital, therefore, to poke your head into a committee room regularly if you hear of a pending unofficial meeting. There are also a myraid of unidentifiable moments when committee work is conducted—perhaps over the phone some night, in the bathroom, or on the way to the key vote. One day a CCAG staff member spied a steady stream of transportation officials moving through a third-floor capitol hallway. Legislators and administrators, state and federal, they all seemed to be gravitating toward a quiet caucus room. Following along, our lobbyist found herself in a high-level strategy meeting on transportation funding, from which the shamefaced public servants chose not to evict her.

YOUR PART IN THE PROCESS: MEMOS

Communicating with legislators is your principal reason for perpetually haunting the capitol. *Talking frequently to legislators is the best way to persuade them of your position;* the importance of this simple method cannot be overstated. Written communication can be an effective supplementary tool, however. Memos spell out your program and leave legislators a sample of your work. We used memos or fact sheets extensively to consolidate information into an easy-reference form that could be readily circulated.

A good legislative memo is simple and short (usually one or two pages), with concise information in an easy-to-read format. Use the tricks of advertising copy — spacing, indenting, underlining, capitalizing—because you may be addressing people with no interest in your issue. Memos should be printed on your letterhead, to keep your organization in legislators' minds. Like a press release a legislative memo should list the name of the person to contact for more information. It helps to adopt or create shorthand references to particular bills or subjects. Everyone at the capitol knew about the "bottle bill."

Make your memo objective and factual. You can conclude with an offer to answer questions.

If at all possible do not simply stuff mailboxes or hand out your materials; talk, however briefly, about your memo as you give it to each person. Ask key legislators later if they have any questions about the memo. A point on protocol: If you are not giving a memo to *every* legislator, be sure to address one to every *essential* person. This means *both* chairpersons, if there are two: A Senate chairperson was miffed that only the House chairperson was addressed on one of our memos.

The Purse Strings

Most measures have some fiscal impact, so the people who control the purse play an integral role in practically everything the legislature does. These people include:

• the governor, who appoints full-time fiscal planners to create fiscal policy

• commissioners and agency heads, who request funds for their departments and programs

• party leaders and committee chairpeople, who set taxing and spending guidelines and ground rules

• the legislature's fiscal analysis staff, who research financial proposals

• other legislators, who individually and collectively negotiate the priorities

• the various lobbies, who apply various pressures

And you need to keep an eye on them all.

More and more legislatures are establishing autonomous offices with permanent nonpartisan professional staff to prepare fiscal impact statements on legislative proposals. Legislatures are trying to develop greater sophistication so they can independently evaluate executive budget and taxation proposals.

Clearly, state policy is closely tied to and reflected in its handling of money matters. Fiscal priorities determine a great many others, and fiscal decisions have far-reaching ramifications. State tax policy is the key to the kind and amount of services the state can provide. So, whether your legislative program relates directly to appropriations and revenue or not, it is essential to have at least a basic understanding of the budget process in the legislature and of how to influence those who have the most to say about fiscal decisions—namely, chairpeople, party leadership, and the governor. On bills affecting cities and towns, local government representatives will have to be reckoned with as well.

Although they tackle genuinely difficult problems of financing and appropriations, a legislature's money committees are also political battlefields. Referring a bill to a money committee, on the pretext that its fiscal impact will be considered, allows legislators and committees to stop the bill and yet escape the blame for blocking it. Traditionally fiscally conservative, these committees are practiced in apologia: "We would like to fund this proposal, but we cannot afford *all* the worthy projects that we might like to support."

When increased costs cannot be avoided, be ready to explain where the money will come from. Find out whether partial or full federal funding is available.

When funds are particularly short in a given year, try to set up your proposal so that its greatest costs arise in later, more-prosperous years. Or draft the bill to take effect a year or two later.

If possible, know what your proposal will cost. Legislators are bound to ask you, and you will look unprepared if you cannot tell them. As with the other aspects of your legislation, be sure you know as much about its fiscal impact as the legislators or committees considering it.

Monitor the drafting of any fiscal impact notes by legislative staff. Be sure the notes are accurate and complete.

Remember: *The time to consider the economic consequences of your proposal is when you first begin,* not in the middle of the session when your bill runs into trouble.

A SPECIALIZED ROLE: DEFENDING YOUR AGENCIES

The money committees hold hearings on the agency budgets proposed by the governor and the agency heads. We felt it appropriate for a citizen group to add its voice to the voices of the advocates sent by departments to defend their requests.

Defending a worthwhile agency is often as important as working for new legislation. Pointing out the shortcomings of an agency in a constructive way is one of the best approaches to helping an agency and the citizens it serves.

Do not assume that agency heads will be effective champions for their departments. Without support from the governor's office, well-intentioned but inexperienced appointees may not be capable of sustaining their requests before an indifferent legislature. Other agency chiefs may actually work to dilute the powers of rival agencies in the struggle for funds.

Newer agencies, especially environmental and consumer protection departments, may come close to being gutted whenever economic straits push government to cut spending. Their services are often considered politically expendable. It may be up to you to convince legislators otherwise.

There is a big difference between eliminating frills and exploiting the "austerity" argument to accomplish short-sighted political ends. In the name of economy, environmental-quality mandates can be weakened and consumer protection laws labeled "unenforceable." Although the bottom line of the budget counts, there are always alternative ways to get to that sum. A public interest group must be able to scrutinize the between-the-lines objective of budget writing.

It is all too easy for hostile legislators and special interest lobbyists to yell "austerity" while chopping away at vital programs. Do not let them get away with it unchallenged. Be ready to expose trumped-up "cost savings" that will actually cost the public plenty.

Do the merits count? The answer is "yes," although you can see by now that merit alone does not win many legislative battles. Your job is to make sure that the merits are considered openly and thoroughly, that the public interest position is clearly heard.

All too often, politics or personalities hold sway. Some

chairpeople, at the hint of any controversy, put off discussion indefinitely or simply refuse to place a bill on the committee agenda.

Vociferous statements by some opinionated members sometimes drown out other members' views. This tactic is used on first-term legislators especially, prefaced with a line like, "When you've been here as long as I have . . ."

Some good bills disappear into the mists because the sponsor never drops a word to the committee or because no one comes to the public hearing. Some bad bills go to the floor because no one bothers to object in committee. Silence is not golden at the legislature. You have got to be heard, speaking up for good legislation and against bad.

In the committee process, as in other parts of the legislative process, there are ways that legislators can appear to discharge obligations without doing anything. Thus, someone will say of a bill he or she sponsored, "I promised I'd put it in — my mayor wanted it — but you can do whatever you want with it," or even ". . . but now I hope you'll forget it." Or a legislator will say, "We ought to draft this bill so they (some clamoring group) can have a public hearing." While getting a bill drafted and introduced is an important first step, it is by no means an indication of real and lasting support.

This penchant for getting off the hook makes certain kinds of bills most appealing, like a bill that lists specific projects as "priorities" but carries no appropriations. A committee can also pass bills knowing the bills would have to get final approval elsewhere — where they are sure to be defeated.

You will find that even though you carefully watch and check everything, events occur in committee that catch you unaware. Hearing dates get changed or set at the very last minute. Bill numbers get changed unexpectedly. After a committee had voted favorably on one of our bills and the meeting had ended, somebody decided to consolidate it with another bill, using the number of the second bill. Meanwhile, we were vainly watching for the original bill number to appear on the calendar. It would have been a long wait.

And then there is the moment when you hear, "This bill has all kinds of problems" (when you thought they had been ironed out in those long sessions last week), and you watch it defeated right under your nose. You have to swallow your disappointment and sally forth, undaunted, to the next bill and the next fight.

SUMMARY

1. Committees are the basic work units of the legislature. They hold hearings, decide the provisions of bills, and decide whether bills reach the floor.

2. Get to know the chairpersons. They have tremendous power.

3. Get to know the committee members. Help them get to know you and your issue.

4. Get to know the staff. They provide an important channel for disseminating your information.

5. Get to know the special interest lobbyists.

6. Committees vary widely in their expertise and efficiency.

7. There are many sources of frustration, including behind-the-scenes dealing, indifference, and inefficiency. You must learn to deal with them.

8. There are always too many committee meetings and too few public interest lobbyists to cover them, but try to attend as many as possible.

9. Committee meetings include regular meetings and voting sessions, conferences, work meetings and seminars, and subcommittee meetings.

10. Informal gatherings are as important as formal committee meetings.

11. Memos explaining your proposals are an important tool. Make them informative but concise. Do not assume that legislators know or even care about your issue.

12. Every proposal can be vulnerable to attack on its claimed fiscal impact, so watch for tactics to defeat your measure in an appropriations or finance committee.

13. Defend the budget and any good programs of the state agency charged with enforcing your laws.

14. Do not depend on merits alone to win your bills; personalities, indifference, old political debts, and unexpected events all may determine the fate of your proposal.

☆ 8 ☆

Public
Hearings

The legislature attempts to meet its obligation to hear public comment by holding hearings on bills before final committee action. Public hearings provide the only opportunity for individuals to appear formally and without invitation to participate in the formulation of legislation. Unfortunately, "the public" rarely appears at public hearings; these forums are more frequently used by lobbyists, state agencies, and other legislators. Therefore, when groups of citizens do participate, their presence can have substantial impact on an issue.

Testimony by a lone individual may be eloquent, but it is not enough. You should present respected experts and demonstrate broad citizen support to insure that legislators will pay close attention to the measures your group is advocating. Getting legislators' attention is the first step toward influencing their votes.

Legislative hearings not only reach legislators, but can also attract potential supporters not yet involved in your issue. *Public hearings, especially if well attended, can become centers of public attention through media coverage.* Good media coverage—which requires preparation on your part—can interest thousands more citizens in what you are trying to accomplish.

Citizen groups cannot approach the amount of money that large corporate interests can spend on lobbying. Northeast Utilities was allotted 14 hours of presentation time at a nuclear power hearing and spent more than $10,000 of the consumers' money; we were given eight hours and spent $30. *Citizen organizing must make up the difference.*

Hearings are important but are only one of the many places citizens need to direct their energy. If these forums take place relatively early in the session, most of what transpires will be forgotten by the time the bills come up for votes. Legislators, like most people, have short memories—unless an indelible mark is made. Such a mark can be left by a vocal or desperate crowd of voters, or a well-reasoned presentation of facts.

If public interest groups could consistently turn out such crowds, things would probably be very different in state capitals. We aim to fill hearing rooms, but such mass confrontations usually occur only when people feel threatened. To arouse vocal public support, you must make clear the urgency of your issue. On those few burning issues whose immediate consequences are easily seen, it is relatively easy to organize citizens for a public hearing—but many, if not most, important issues do not lend themselves so easily to massive public demonstrations. Often, *you* have to establish public awareness of unrecognized issues. *You* may have to arouse the public's interest. Many significant bills have neither magnetism for the public nor glamour for the legislature. The importance of regulating debt collectors or assigning top priority to mass transportation projects is in no way diminished because few people have so far clamored for reform. At first you may be the *only* person speaking against the collection agencies or the highway lobby—which is why it is so important that you be there.

PREPARATION

We have stressed the importance of framing your issues to attract broad-based support. Public hearings, valuable primarily for the publicity they can help you generate inside and outside the legislature, are the place to demonstrate the strength of that support. Plan your media strategy as carefully as your testimony. (Review the chapter on the press for more details.)

Using a public hearing effectively takes solid advance planning, starting perhaps months before the hearing. Look for organizations that have been active on similar legislation in the past, as they are likely to be both competent and willing. Contact others with political influence: union representatives, professionals, academicians, public officials, and other community leaders.

Know the ground rules before the hearing begins. (Having a working relationship with the committee clerk or chairperson helps.) Verify the exact time, date, and place of the hearing, the bill to be discussed, whether there will be a time limit, whether there will be questioning by other participants, and what format will be used (for example, debate, panel discussion, individual testimony). Identify, when possible, the opposing speakers. Find out what audio-visual equipment is available, the layout of the room, and, always, the likelihood of press coverage (check for other major events that may preempt your coverage). Find out how the speaking order is determined; if there is a list, get on it as soon as possible.

Finding Witnesses

Be sure to meet with potential witnesses whose testimony you seek. Not all experts have the talents to effectively challenge the opposition. Consider these qualifications:

1. area of expertise and credentials
2. style and demeanor
3. political influence and reputation

If your witness is deficient in the first or second area, he or she may turn out to be more of a liability than an asset.

Remember that you are probably the expert on your political strategies. Do not be so awed by credentials that you fail to coach your witnesses on the receptiveness of your legislators and the best approaches to win them over. Make every effort to discusss strategy with your witnesses — *long before* the hearing.

You can seek witnesses with political influence instead of technical knowledge. Such persons might be labor representatives, members of Congress, state and local officials, community leaders, prominent business people, or professionals in related fields. The appearance of the president of a large local union or a U.S. senator may have a favorable impact even if the testimony is little more than a subjective endorsement.

Solicit letters to the committee from influential individuals who cannot be at the hearing. These efforts are well worth the time. In one ambitious effort we arranged for five Nobel laureates and six other eminent scientists to send letters to a committee. Our press release on the letters got front-page coverage in Hartford.

Remember that some constituents, particularly political contributors and community or media leaders, get special attention from legislators. People who would normally be expected to oppose a position but who testify in favor — business leaders advocating strong consumer or environment legislation, party regulars supporting government accountability — make especially effective lobbyists.

Doing the Legwork

When you solicit the support of others on your issues, be ready to do extra laps if necessary. You will often have to provide facts and figures to nonexperts, or help write testimony for inexperienced or hesitant allies. We found this especially important when citizen lobbyists spoke at local hearings around the state that CCAG staff did not attend. By helping them with their testimony, we assured consistency in the presentation of information — not to mention more people willing to get up and present it.

Line up your experts sufficiently far in advance, and plan to get maximum mileage out of their visit. You might arrange a press conference, press interviews, sessions with key officials, or other public appearances.

Local Hearings

Sometimes hearings are scheduled around the state for those people who cannot trek up to the state capital. Some committees hold local hearings *and* hearings in the capital. Do not be afraid to request or demand local hearings, especially on a subject that particularly affects one area. Such requests are hard to refuse, as legislators do not want to appear irresponsible or unwilling to make the effort to broaden citizen participation.

Local hearings often cover many more bills at one time, attract fewer lobbyists, and adhere less strictly to protocol. Because there are generally few legislators present, this may be a good opportunity to pin down a legislator on his positions on a number of special bills.

Try to find a key person in the district who will not only speak, but also pull in others for the hearing. If legislators are already hearing from you in the capital, it will add to your effectiveness to have *other* constituents give testimony locally. You can help, of course. Feed your contact person as much information as you can about the legislator, the events and reactions during hearings in the capital, questions and key points to play up or play down. If they wish, you should help write testimony for participants. Your most important role may be to assist in publicizing the hearing in the local media in order to get a large turnout and good coverage of the issue.

Writing Testimony

Do not let memories of old Perry Mason episodes convince you that testimony must be stiff and formal. It should not be. Public hearing testimony is basically a short speech — and, as in any other speech, if you bore your audience, you will not get your message across. You must be brief, simple, and clear. Eschew obfuscation (in plain English, avoid confusion).

As you write, remember that you will be *speaking* the words you write (more or less). Long words that look impressive in print may sound terrible when spoken.

Do not fake expertise. If you begin your testimony trying to sound like a nuclear engineer you will regret it when a sharp legislator starts asking technical questions.

AT THE HEARING

Come Early and Get Good Seats

You want to speak early — before you and the audience get tired, before the legislators drift off to other events, and before the reporters leave to write their stories. You want good seats so that you can hear — and prepare to respond to — other speakers. Of course, there is no guarantee that the committee members will even attend the hearing, or stay for more than ten minutes. You may want to ask key legislators to come so that they can hear your testimony. But do not be surprised if you find yourself speaking to a recording machine and one legislator — or if you find legislators being allowed to speak before you, regardless of sign-up sheets and arrival times.

Bring written copies of your testimony. Distribute copies to members of the committee and to members of the press. By giving copies to the recording secretary, you ensure that your statement becomes part of the permanent record.

Keep in mind that you may be the first citizen to speak; this has symbolic as well as practical importance. Your performance may be valuable for any negotiations that follow, and may help guarantee that you will not be left out of sessions where final drafts of bills are determined. Individual legislators may come to you during the hearing to ask if the opposition is telling it straight, and, if not, what questions can be asked to point up inaccuracies. Always be alert to the reactions of legislators and other participants; you should be able to pick up clues about how the various viewpoints are being received.

If you have lined up several speakers, you may want to disperse them throughout the hearing schedule. Because committee members may wander in and out during the hearing, this may give more of them a chance to hear your side. It also provides some flexibility to rebut testimony if necessary.

During the hearing you and your allies must remain courteous at all times. This does not mean, however, that you must remain silent when it is appropriate to speak up or raise questions.

Delivering the Testimony

Talk to your listeners; do not *read* your prepared statement word for word. Your tone and delivery determine whether anyone listens to you or understands you. When you know your subject, you can be much more convincing if you speak rather than read. You can also exercise flexibility in answering newly raised questions or arguments of previous speakers. Emphasize your main points. Do not be repetitious; do not cover so many minor points that nobody remembers your major one.

Use audio-visual aids to present complicated data. Enlarged charts and tables, slides, photos, and films are often used in clarifying complex issues.

Address specific sections of legislation so that committee members can refer to the bill as you speak. When you can, propose alternative language to correct problems you see in the bill. Stress such positive facets as economic benefits to consumers and business, social and political impact, and environmental benefit. Keep in mind that, as they are listening to you, legislators may be thinking, "If I go along with this person, how will it help me?" Make your pitch accordingly.

The Underhanded

We found ourselves in an unexpected situation when two

of our expert witnesses at a nuclear power hearing were challenged on the basis of their appearance and age. A utility company spokesman from California began, "Gentlemen, just look at what we have here. At that end of the table there is a lot of hair. Those two gentlemen are young and idealistic. They do not have a reasonable perspective on this issue because they are inexperienced in the area in which they are testifying. Now look at this end of the table. You've got old balding men who have a much broader perspective on how nuclear power fits into the scheme of things."

Our two hairy young men were in fact nationally respected experts on nuclear power, and one of them had been highly praised a few years earlier by one of the balding experts at the other end of the table.

Planting doubt through unfounded accusations or claims is often effective. It is the kind of low tactic that you should not engage in but that you may be subjected to. False or misleading testimony, even if later retracted, raises suspicions that muddy the issue and undermine the case. During a hearing on the bottle bill, an industry representative declared that more than 1,000 jobs would be lost if the bill were passed. The statement drew wide press coverage. The lobbyist later revised his figures downward, closer to our estimate of 250, but no comparable publicity was given the correction and nothing could have erased the impact of that original forceful misrepresentation.

You will not always have the opportunity to publicly refute inaccurate data or false allegations, but your own statistics should be recent, reliable, and not misleading. If you cannot reply publicly to damaging claims, at least notify key persons and friendly legislators. When one legislator loudly accused us of misrepresenting a commissioner's stand on a controversial bill, that commissioner wrote him a letter to set the matter straight, and sent copies to several other key legislators. Be prepared to spend time defending yourself or your allies from cheap shots. Your reputation and your information must be able to hold up under fire.

The Personal Touch

Some people would say that holding up a rubber dollar and stretching it across the room to illustrate what state employees are obliged to do with their paychecks is a ridiculous way to make a point. Still, good gimmicks can help sell ideas. Use your imagination to find ways to impress a legislator's memory. There was the witness who pulled a can of baked beans out of a grocery bag to complain about computer price-marking systems. Legislators longing for an overdue lunch expressed uncommon interest in the beans.

Another approach is to appeal to the legislator's conscience, a technique long ago perfected by trial lawyers. Encourage people from affected groups to testify personally on legislation: young children speaking about child abuse or the rights of minors, the elderly explaining shortcomings of state medical assistance, disabled persons asking for access ramps in all new public facilities, lung patients testifying on how air pollution affects them. These appearances are not soon forgotten.

After You Testify

Besides coming early, you should stay late, until the hearing is over. Stick around to answer any questions, to hear any responses to your testimony, and in general to keep an eye on the proceedings. Questions about a bill may — and probably will — be raised *after* you finish testimony.

Follow-up is essential. If you bring citizens to the capitol, encourage them to speak to their own representatives and senators as constituents. Take advantage of the momentum a public hearing can offer to keep the issue in the legislator's mind. Urge supporters and citizen lobbyists to follow up the hearings with phone calls and letters to their legislators, and letters to editors of local newspapers.

SUMMARY

1. Public hearings are the major (and too often unused) channels for public participation in the formulation of legislation.

2. *Broad citizen support and expert testimony are your two best ways to make an impact.*

3. *Planning—mobilizing people to attend, locating experts, getting press coverage—must begin well in advance. Coordinating these various efforts must continue throughout.*

4. *Be sure that your experts know not only the subject but how to present their case effectively to these legislators.*

5. *Be ready to counter underhanded tactics, such as planting doubts about your witnesses' expertise.*

6. *Nonexperts with political influence are also very effective at public hearings.*

7. *Capitalize on all aspects of hearings.*

8. *Try to be at the hearing from start to finish. Testifying early is usually an advantage.*

9. *Use your imagination to deliver interesting testimony.*

☆ 9 ☆

Negotiations

Legislators often struggle to make everyone happy. That is no easy task. Whatever the issue there are *at least* two sides, and someone is usually unhappy with the outcome. To minimize this unhappiness legislators often involve representatives of differing views in the drafting of legislation. To be one of the representatives, *you* must take the first step. You have to establish yourself as a representative of a viewpoint that should be taken into account. Your full-time participation in the process and your skill at citizen mobilization provide your legitimacy. Once legislators come to see your group as one with integrity, accurate information, and public support, you may find yourself being invited to participate in more negotiating meetings than you want to. Until then you will have to utilize whatever opportunities you can. Try to attend important negotiating sessions even if you are not invited. Your presence alone can have an impact.

Negotiating does not always refer to opponents glaring at each other across a table trying to win concessions by intimidation. If you are pushing a bill to ban construction of nuclear power plants, do not expect to meet with a reactor manufacturer's lobbyist and iron out a neat little compromise; the difference in positions is too vast. You are more likely to be involved in negotiations with people who are allies to some extent or who are uncommitted. A legislator may feel that a bill you have asked him to introduce goes too far; he might then ask you to meet with him and his staff, and perhaps another interested legislator and her staff, to negotiate a compromise. Or you might negotiate with a legislator or another lobbyist who supports or is at least sympathetic to the motives behind your proposal, but strongly objects to one provision.

Whoever you are negotiating with, start with written words, not spoken ones. The time for vague, "Hey, I have an idea for a bill" meetings is *before* the legislative session. By now you should have a draft—preferably yours—to work with. Otherwise your "negotiating" session will turn into a philosophical debate on vague ideas. With all participants holding a copy of draft legislation in front of them, your meeting can do what it is designed to: reach agreement on specific provisions.

Before starting a negotiating session, your side should have a clear idea of your position, including possible compromises, points beyond compromise, and suggested alternative drafts. Nothing is worse than trying to figure out your stand in front of your opposition. If a new suggestion takes you by surprise, a brief caucus by your team is usually acceptable.

Decide how to present your case *before* the meeting. You can negotiate in a straightforward manner by immediately presenting a compromise that is acceptable to you, or you can offer an extreme position from which you are willing to bargain. The nature of the issue and the relative strength of your side and the opposition should determine the approach. Taking an extreme position opens you to the charge of insincerity and may convince the other side that there is no reason to negotiate. Starting out with a compromise may lead the other side to think you can be pushed much further.

In the heady atmosphere of all this wheeling and dealing, do not forget: Always act in good faith. Do not agree to something and then change your mind later. If you must consult other members of your group before making a final commitment (try hard to avoid this), say so; it is better to delay things a bit than to back out of commitments. Even the vaguest implication of behind-the-scenes politicking after reaching a negotiated agreement will open you up to charges of acting in bad faith. A bad reputation is more quickly established than a good one, and can make it almost impossible for you to work with any legislators. A reputation for dealing in good faith will make legislators more likely to turn to you for information or support.

When legislators *do* turn to you, do not be too flattered to be a bit skeptical. You may be window dressing; having a public interest representative involved in something looks great. If you are the only public interest lobbyist invited to a negotiating session with a dozen of the smoothest-talking lawyers in town, representing the state's largest industries, beware—it may be a trap. During debate on the bill, the sponsor can hint at broad public support for it: "I worked with (your group) on this bill from the beginning. They helped draft it."

Negotiating is an art. Some people make a big thing of where negotiations take place (your territory vs. their territory vs. neutral ground) and of matching or outnumbering the other side. But these concerns are usually far less important than your self-confidence, your familiarity with the problems and with alternative solutions, and the validity of your position. Always argue on the basis of logic and examples. Heavy-handed power moves ("If you don't agree, we won't help the bill") go over like lead balloons and are not appropriate for most citizen groups. *Argue the merits and back your stance with citizen clout later.*

If possible, your negotiating team should have at least one lawyer. Wording legislation can be very tricky, and your wording may even be turned against you if it is interpreted incorrectly. If you are unable to afford legal assistance, in some states you can turn to a consumer counsel office. (Depending on the state, these lawyers may deal with a narrow or wide range of issues, such as public utilities or environmental or consumer protection.) Legal-services attorneys are also natural allies on many consumer issues.

Be prepared to give in on some points. You may be so deeply committed to your issue that you feel it is dishonorable —selling out—to agree to any weakening of your proposal. But to refuse to budge may be to doom yourself to getting nothing. If you are not willing to change a letter of your original draft, do not bother sitting down to negotiate.

While compromise can be distasteful, it is often vital to give the other side a stake in the bill. But if you are uncomfortable with a compromise, do not feel obligated to accept it. Be sure you are agreeing to a bill that you feel is worthwhile, because you will be bound to it.

If you are negotiating, even at the request of a legislator, it is perfectly respectable to fail to reach a compromise. You can suggest to the committee that it is better to have no bill at all than to pass a poor compromise, or you can submit alternative drafts on the disputed areas.

After a negotiating session, always volunteer. Volunteer to redraft, to consolidate agreed changes, to deliver the final product, or to do any other important tasks that need doing. There are almost always slight ambiguities or issues not completely resolved after complex negotiations. You want to be the one who settles them—still keeping in the bounds of good faith, of course. The extra effort will almost always pay off in getting bills a little closer to the way you want them.

Bargaining for neutrality, the next best thing after support, is quite common and can be very effective where you have properly sized up the balance of forces on an issue. Not everybody will like your bill; you are trying to keep down the numbers of those who dislike it. Lobbyists caught up in the day-to-day excitement of the legislative session risk losing sight of the long-term value of their bills.

You must decide what are the essential parts of your bill that simply cannot be compromised. On our bill creating a task force to examine nuclear power questions, we had decided that the critical issue was setting up the panel, not listing in the bill the specific topics for study. Therefore we agreed to eliminate one or two specifics in the bill so that the utilities would not oppose the measure. The bill passed, the task force was set up, and, as one of its first acts, decided that its subject matter was unlimited.

SUMMARY

1. Try to participate in negotiations on bills you are interested in.

2. Always act in good faith.

3. Periodically reexamine your bill; do not negotiate away its vital components.

4. Prepare for a negotiating session so that you know where to draw the line. Establish which points cannot be compromised and which allow you some leeway. Have a working outline and a draft of your revised bill.

☆ **10** ☆

Lobbying
the Floor

After months of hard work on a bill; you have persuaded enough legislators to get it out of committee. Now what?

Start all over again. Only this time, you must sell the entire legislature on the idea.

Where do you begin? Start by thinking about the nature of your legislation, its complexity, its reception in previous legislative sessions, and the relative power of its backers and detractors. These are all crucial points in formulating your strategy.

THE NATURE OF YOUR ISSUE

Most public interest issues fall into one of three areas, each of which requires a different approach:

1. Broad proposals introduced in the legislature for the first time. Example: a ban on nuclear power plant construction. This type of bill is usually vigorously opposed by the affected interest groups. Legislators tend to have little understanding of the proposal—although they may, like other people, have many preconceived biases based on little factual knowledge. You will have to do a lot of educational work on these issues. They are too bold, too controversial (sometimes thought to be

too radical) for you to rely on legislators following the lead of a few influential lawmakers—who may also be difficult to convince. The outcome of these bills in their first year or two is usually some kind of formal defeat: compromise, negotiations, interim study committees (that is, delay), or a simple overwhelming negative vote.

If you are pushing this type of bill, be prepared to spend a few years fighting for it—and to overhaul it many times along the way. Part of the role of a public interest organization is to introduce new ideas. An unsuccessful lobbying effort can be a solid basis for winning in the future.

2. Perennial issues that still generate persistent opposition. Example: a generic drug bill that was first introduced two years ago, creating little public interest but massive industry opposition, and is now beginning to enjoy strong public support. Opposition from vested interests remains strong, but continuing efforts at passage are reaching the public, which is putting pressure on legislators for action.

Lobbying efforts on these issues should be concentrated primarily on influential legislators and secondarily on the rank and file. For the most part, basic understanding of the concept is no longer lacking. You now have to overcome opposition arguments.

3. Uncontroversial, technical bills that are nevertheless important and progressive. Refinements in landlord/tenant law and improvements in court procedures are examples of issues of public importance that are often too detailed and subtle to generate wide attention.

The fate of such legislation is often in the hands of a small group of committee chairpeople, knowledgeable committee members, and legislators with special interests for or against the bill. After compromises and negotiations with this select few, they will normally guide the bill over any remaining legislative obstacles.

The powers that be. Before you start an intensive floor

effort on a bill, you must realistically assess its chances for passage. Consider the following:

1. the position taken by the governor, relevant state agencies, and the majority party leadership (minority party also if it holds enough seats to make a difference)
2. the power and degree of organized opposition
3. the degree of visible public support
4. support from local and statewide media, especially big-city newspapers, television, and radio; prospects for obtaining further media attention
5. the degree of commitment and involvement of other organizations that support the legislation
6. the cost of the legislation
7. the past effectiveness of your lobbying

The Governor and the Legislative Leaders

Do not assume that the governor and the leadership know that your bill exists. It is your job to make them aware. We always distributed a list of our legislative priorities to the governor and all legislators, but that is not enough. Try to meet with the governor (or at least with a high-ranking aide) and with the leaders to discuss your bill.

If you are unable to arrange these meetings, go to your legislative allies—the chairperson of the committee that approved the bill, interested committee members, or other legislators who support the proposal—and ask them to lobby the legislative leaders or governor's staff for you. Particularly if you have bipartisan support, contact the leaders of both parties.

The feedback you receive from these efforts should let you know if leadership plans to take a position on your issue. Do not get too carried away by a position response; make sure you know exactly what the leaders have agreed to do. Leaders' degree of commitment spans a wide range: they may say they will actively push the issue, agree to mention it favorably in caucus, or give you their word that they will not oppose the bill. Declining to take a position may be a camouflage to hide outright opposition. If your legislation is on the majority party's campaign platform, it may not have much trouble, but do not take that for granted. Legislators have notoriously short memories when it comes to inconvenient campaign promises.

If the leaders oppose you, you can turn their own tactics against them by emphasizing to rank-and-file legislators the importance of voting their conscience and not blindly following party bigwigs.

Once you know the governor's and the leadership's positions you can proceed to develop an appropriate lobbying strategy. Even with leadership support, you need to make sure that the opposition does not patch together enough minority party opponents and majority party defectors to beat you.

Tactics

There are a variety of ways bills can be pushed — or quietly maneuvered — through the legislature and onto the governor's desk.

Tiptoeing is one option. Alert only those people who have to know, such as the leaders, committee members, chairpeople, and very interested legislators; then calmly and gently guide the bill through the paces. Remember that most controversial bills fail the first time around. If your bill has not attracted any strong, organized opposition, avoid engaging in heated debate with special interests who might otherwise neglect the issue.

This is particularly true of highly technical bills sponsored by committee chairpeople, bills that may not be fully understood by every legislator. An obscure technical bill and a respected sponsor (preferably chairperson of the relevant committee) can be a powerful combination. "I don't know exactly what the bill does, but it's Charlie's bill and he knows this stuff; I trust him," might be a typical legislator's reaction.

Most bills that public interest groups push, however, are not the types that go unnoticed.

On CCAG's controversial legislation—that is, most of our bills—our lobbyists contacted key legislators first. If time allowed and a broader base of support was necessary, we approached other legislators. Leadership support—on those rare occasions when we had it—was not enough to guarantee a bill's passage. We had to get out in the capitol halls and lobbies to present the bill to the rank-and-file.

The extent of lobbying activity. The time you spend lobbying after a favorable committee report depends on your workload. If you are working on one bill you may have weeks to contact all the legislators. But if you are trying to watch four or five bills at once, you may have only a few days to lobby the same number of legislators. We used the following system working from the top as far down as we had time to go:

1. Determine which leaders still need persuading. Work on them first.

2. List the members of the committee reporting out the bill according to support, opposition, or neutrality. Start lining up supporters to handle the floor debate. Then lobby those who have not taken a strong position, including moderate opponents. Start keeping a tally of supporters and opponents.

3. Make a list of all legislators, with notations on party membership, whether they are influential, the position they have taken on your issue, and who in your group knows each member. Divide the legislators among the number of lobbyists available to you. Each lobbyist (or you, if you are the sole lobbyist) should personally contact legislators on a priority basis: influential lawmakers first, active majority party legislators next, then remaining members of the majority or active minority members (depending on the partisan nature of the issue), and finally any remaining legislators.

4. As contacts are made and positions determined, keep a running tally of supporters, opponents, and undecideds. If it looks as if the vote will be close, renew your efforts at the

undecided legislators—especially those who are influential. Keep your ear to the ground for new arguments by the opposition; develop counterarguments. Get those counterarguments to friendly legislators and the bill's major supporters. Do not always contact every legislator to counter every new opposition argument; you will just give more credibility to the opposing charges. Let other legislators do the job of defusing new arguments. Naturally, if directly asked by any legislator, provide your defense.

When you are dealing with numerous bills, each lobbyist (if you have more than one) should be assigned to a major issue but should know all the other issues as well. It is almost impossible for a lobbyist to talk to every legislator. Instead, each lobbyist talks to a group of legislators on several issues. This allows personal working relationships to be established. Legislators may rely on the lobbyist assigned to them to answer questions on any of your bills. Keep informed about all of them.

It is important to coordinate your visits to a legislator. You do not want more than one lobbyist visiting the same legislator in a single day. Moreover, you do not want every group that is working on an issue with you to make separate visits to the same legislator and make the same arguments.

As we have suggested previously, a brief memo summarizing the bill and the reasons for your position is invaluable in approaching and lobbying legislators.

First contacts. Ideally, lobbyists work with only a small circle of people they know very well. Industry lobbyists in Washington and in many state capitols operate this way; they are rarely seen buttonholing legislators in the halls. As new public interest lobbyists, however, you will approach legislators whom you have never met before. Immediately swinging into a song and dance proclaiming the merits of your bill to a newly met legislator may be uncomfortable at first, but most legislators are accustomed to being cornered by lobbyists.

Some expect it, and others may even be flattered by your attention.

Chasing the elusive legislator. You will soon become used to approaching the legislators. A more serious problem can be knowing where to track them down. Some states, like Connecticut, lack the facilities to give each legislator an office. Some legislators are rarely in their offices. Chasing them about and searching odd corners may make you feel eight years old, but it is critical to your success. Your job is to find them.

• When voting sessions are about to begin, or are temporarily recessed, your quarry can often be found in the lobby outside the chamber (the origin of the word "lobbyist").

• Legislators like to be near the center of power; party leadership offices are good stalking grounds.

• Chairpeople and legislators focusing on one committee may be in their committee meeting rooms.

• Station yourself near legislators' mailboxes. Wait outside bathrooms (if you want legislators' full attention, it is best to catch them on the way *out*). Bars, coffee machines, cafeterias, and the like offer places to persuade legislators for the duration of a meal or a drink.

The approach. Your first lobbying contacts with unfamiliar legislators will probably be brief. Often you will have time only to blurt out your name, your organization, and the issue you are working on. Try to hand over your memo on your legislation before the legislator hurries away. While it may seem disappointing, this initial encounter is important. It may prove to be the only opportunity to talk to certain legislators.

You need to refine your presentation to gear it to the individual legislators. You should have done enough background study on the legislator to figure a way to emphasize those aspects of your issue that may strike a responsive chord.

Start with the legislator's agenda, not yours. Each lawmaker has his or her own interests and friends, and each listens most attentively to his or her own constituency. Does the legislator owe his or her election to labor support? If the lawmaker always votes on an issue on the basis of jobs, there is no sense giving a long exhortation on the beneficial energy savings of a bill. To urban legislators we emphasized the benefits elderly citizens would derive from being able to compare prescription drug prices if pharmacies were required to post prices. To legislators who had nuclear plants in their districts, we emphasized constituent fears when we discussed a nuclear safety commission. To leadership we pointed out the benefits they and their party could expect at election time for their open support of significant consumer or environmental bills during the session.

Develop stages to your presentation, so that you do not find yourself rattling on so long that the legislator stops listening. Be self-assured and businesslike. You need to impress the legislator with your manner as well as your arguments.

Lobbyists must be very aggressive, sometimes almost brash. Shyness and evident nervousness will hurt you. You need to spy a legislator heading down a hall and instantly move to intercept, formulating a presentation in a matter of seconds. Use good judgment in making these approaches: Being aggressive does not mean being rude and interrupting a discussion, but just because a legislator is walking hurriedly or looks harried is no reason to back away. If legislators are too busy to talk, they usually let you know—perhaps abruptly, but usually without rancor.

If you close in on a legislator on the move, offer to walk along and present your issue in motion. Passing memos to a legislator who has reached full stride can be a tricky operation, but can be perfected with practice. Capture attention by emphasizing only the main points of your legislation.

If something you mention is of interest to a legislator, he or she may stop in his tracks and continue the discussion. More often, however, he is preoccupied with his destination, and may not hear a word you say. The legislator will give you a wave of the hand and rush off with an echoing cry of, "Get back to me later when I've got more time." You will wonder if it was worth it, but you *have* established initial contact, a memo *was* delivered (and *may* be read), and the legislator *may* remember you and identify you with the right bill.

Do not assume that legislators will contact you with questions or comments. Follow up yourself whenever the opportunity arises. Memorize legislator's faces and do not let lawmakers pass you without using the chance to talk to them again, or at least remind them of who you are and where they know you from.

Measuring the response. While making your presentation, you will need to split your attention between what *you* are saying and how the *legislator* is responding. Is he listening, does he appear preoccupied or rushed, is he following your arguments as you talk? Give the legislator a chance to ask questions. You can usually tell from these questions how knowledgeable he is on the subject. A legislator's questions may also give you an indication of how to guide the discussion.

If your presentation is received with silence or blank stares, do not simply retreat; ask some questions yourself. But be cautious. Do not ask, "Why didn't you support this last year?" Instead try, "We've had quite a few citizen complaints on this problem; have you heard from your constituents?" You can then go on to illustrate the points of your bill with the complaints *you* have heard.

If you are overwhelmed with a barrage of questions, you at least know that you have struck a responsive chord. Answering questions, even the hostile ones, gives you the opportunity to reemphasize your main points. Through this question-and-answer process the outlines of the legislator's position gradually become clear. In some cases legislators take clear-cut positions: "I'm going to vote against this crazy bill because . . ." But often they hem and haw, express various doubts and reservations, or say that they are leaning one way or another.

Legislative smokescreens. Sometimes legislators try to make you feel as if you are asking for personal favors when you lobby. It is dangerous to allow a legislator to hold this opinion. When lobbying legislators, stress the importance of your bill to the citizens affected, not your personal appreciation of support.

A time-honored tactic of some legislators and opposition lobbyists is to confuse the issue with smokescreens. They may try to intimidate you as a citizen lobbyist, with technical or professional jargon or with citations of their vast experience in the area. The implication usually is that you are not qualified to be seeking this legislation or making your arguments. Often the first question by legislators who are attorneys is: "Have you studied law?" If you have not, make sure you can say truthfully that you have had an attorney work with you on it, and that if the legislator has any technical questions about the bill, you can get an answer. Do not hang your head over not being able to cite any professional expertise. Remind legislators, if necessary, that citizens have a right to participate in the legislative process and that you are respresenting nonexpert citizens.

Legislators may also try to lead you off onto a tangent. Some legislators, seemingly out of natural curiosity, will ask where you come from. That is fine, but after a few minutes of "Why, that's a nice town; I've been there many times; how long have you lived there?" the legislator may suddenly say "I've got to run" just as you were about to mention your bill.

Another common stall sounds like this: "Well, before we can consider a bill like this, we have to address the whole question of . . ." There follows a long elucidation of some age-old fundamental philosophical dilemma that will probably never be resolved. Again, after a few minutes of conversation, you realize that you have not discussed your bill and the legislator is hurrying off down the hall.

Do not let this happen to you. When a legislator begins to wander, politely but firmly steer the conversation back to your legislation. You must make legislators realize that your time is as valuable as theirs, and you cannot afford to waste it. A certain amount of nonlegislative chatter helps develop a friendly relationship, but if the only time you have to talk to a legislator is a few minutes in the hall between meetings, *do not waste it.* You may not have another chance to talk to this legislator until it is too late.

Seizing opportunities. Lobbyists who come to know legislators well can vary their lobbying approaches depending on individual quirks and inside information.

A CCAG lobbyist had learned that a senator was particularly angry at the governor for opposing one of his bills. When a crucial vote on an important antienvironmental bill came up, our lobbyist casually informed the senator that the governor really wanted the bill to go through. The senator's eyes lit up and a smile appeared on his face. The senator, not known for any environmental concern, cast the deciding vote against the governor and for the state's environmental interests.

Keeping in Close Touch with Sponsors

Always maintain close contact with your bill's chief legislative supporters. If you keep a tally sheet or head count as you lobby individual legislators, pass this information along to the legislators providing your chief support. They can be influential in persuading uncommitted legislators.

When you have identified the swing votes in the legislature, ask yourself again how you can influence them to vote your way. Examine uncommitted legislators' districts. Do you have supporters or sympathetic organizations there who can pressure the legislators? Can you use some recent event, new study, or other development to help push the undecideds into the "yes" column? Do not give up until you get firm "yes" or "no" commitments.

Lobbying the Other Chamber

Few public interest groups have the resources to lobby both houses of a legislature simultaneously. Concentrate on one house at a time. A favorable attitude in the Senate will do you little good if the House defeats the bill before it gets there. However, as you scramble to contact all the key legislators in one chamber, do not lose sight of the lobbying effort that awaits you — *if* your bill passes — in the other chamber.

Do not assume that the attitudes of one chamber will be reflected in the other one. For some reason, consumer issues seemed to fare better in the Connecticut House and human rights issues better in the Senate. This might have been because the Senate was much smaller than the House, making it easier for special interest lobbyists fighting consumer legislation to contact the members of that chamber. The smaller the chamber, the easier it is for you (and other lobbyists) to reach each of the legislators.

Once again, though, the intensity of your lobbying efforts will depend on the nature of your issue and its opposition. If your legislation is opposed by a powerful interest group, such as utility companies or major manufacturing industries, the odds are fairly good that *they* will be lobbying both chambers at the same time. In some legislative situations, members of one chamber may decide it is senseless to pass a bill if the second chamber's leaders are already convinced the bill should fail. Lobbyists who are able to convince the second chamber in this fashion may well steal the march. Your ear should be close enough to the ground to pick up signs of this happening, so that you can direct your efforts toward countering the opposition.

Party Caucus

The party caucus is a meeting where the members of a political party in one chamber discuss strategy, debate issues, and sometimes establish a unified party position on legislation about to come to the floor. This unified position, of course, is the objective of the caucus from leadership's point of view.

Because of the privacy of the caucus (they are usually closed to the public), the discussions are often freewheeling and emotional. Party members let their hair down to push their bills, ask questions, and air their gripes. (Better here than in public, leadership figures.) Many times, floor debate and final voting merely ratify decisions already made in caucus. This is particularly true when one party is a dominant majority and takes cohesive positions. CCAG was fortunate to be able to sit in on most Senate Democratic caucuses.

If you are shut out. The Senate caucus was open to us because we insisted for years that caucuses should not be closed to the public. A worthwhile objective for public interest groups is to exert enough pressure to open up the caucuses. But that may take a while, and if the caucuses in your state are closed, you will naturally have to depend on your inside contacts to keep you informed on caucus deliberations. Bills in Connecticut are usually discussed in caucus the day that they become eligible for floor action. Refer to your House or Senate calendars and keep in close touch with your legislative contacts. They will probably be able to tell you when the caucus will review your legislation. Be sure your sponsors and supporters are thoroughly briefed on the bill so they can push or defend it within their party caucus. Meet with them afterwards to find out how the discussion went.

Pitfalls and Stratagems

A favorable report by a committee does not necessarily mean that your bill will speedily reach the floor intact for an up or down vote. And once the bill makes it to the calendar, that does not mean you can concentrate only on persuading legislators on the merits of the bill. Potential obstacles still remain. Here are some to watch for.

Second and third readings. In most states, bills go through stages referred to as "first reading," "second reading," and "third reading." (The terminology dates from the days before modern printing and photocopying techniques, when bills were read aloud three times before being voted on.)

The first reading theoretically occurs when the bill is

introduced and referred to committee—nothing to worry about there. A bill is "on second reading" after it is reported out from committee. In some states, the bill simply appears on the second reading calendar for one day—during which it cannot be voted on—and then automatically moves to third reading and eligibility for floor action the next day. (Thus the second reading calendar warns you in advance of what bills will be coming up for votes.)

In other states, a bill is debated, amended, and voted on while it is on second reading—and then, *if* the vote is favorable, *sent back to the rules committee,* from which it must emerge and survive *another* floor vote (on third reading) to pass.

Legislative staff review. The first stop for most bills after a favorable committee report is a checkpoint known in Connecticut as the Legislative Commissioner's Office (LCO). It may be known by another name in your state, but you probably have a legislative department that performs the same functions. In this office, usually controlled by the majority party, staff lawyers review recently approved committee bills. They tighten up the statutory language of the committee version, check its constitutionality, and make sure it does not conflict with existing laws.

As the bill goes through this routine checkup, its substance *should* remain unchanged. If all goes according to the book, you should still be able to recognize the bill, save for minor repairs, as the same one you have been working on. The LCO staff members are not elected officials with official power to amend or delete substance. They are appointed to perform rather straightforward technical tasks.

Politics being what it is, however, provisions *are* sometimes changed and sections *do* disappear. Watch for this and be prepared to fight if it happens to your bill.

Countering foul play. What can be done about power plays? If your bill seems to encounter serious delays on its way to the floor, use your contacts—committee chairpeople, influential legislators, committee staff—to find out where the problem is. Ask any of your powerful legislative friends to check on your bill and get it moving again. You may be able to do much of the checking yourself if you have good contacts in the administrative staff of your legislature. But if there seem to be potentially fatal difficulties facing your bill, rely on a legislator for assistance. If you can find out the objection, you may be able to offer a saving compromise, but you may already have been outmaneuvered by the opposition. Your bill may have been transformed into a useless proposal. You may need to send out word that you are withdrawing support of the bill.

You also have the option, if any hope remains for your bill, of going to the press with your story. In serious cases of treachery, you may want to launch a public media campaign against your oppostion. If your legislation was attacked through an unethical and probably illegal circumvention of the legislative process—say so. If appropriate, call for formal action by the legislature's internal ethics body.

The time to contact friendly legislators is when there seems a realistic chance that, with pressure, your bill might still be released with most of its important sections intact. Urge your legislative supporters to apply pressure. Legislative leaders are also good barometers. If they are noncommittal in response to your pleas, then you are not likely to win.

Sending the bill back to committee. One device often used (usually by leadership) to defeat a bill is to send it back to committee— either by recommitting it to the committee from which it came or referring it to another committee. Such a move usually comes after committee reporting deadlines are past, meaning the bill cannot get out again. It is very difficult to fight this kind of maneuver. To be able to stop it, you must know ahead of time that such a move is coming. If you do not have a strong proponent of your bill willing to fight recommittal or referral, then the bill can be quietly defeated in a few seconds.

Letting the clock run out. Especially in those states that have a legal deadline for ending the session, this is a favorite leadership tactic. If the end of the session is nearing and your bill has not been acted on, start asking why.

SUMMARY

1. *Begin gathering information and support for the floor vote long before your bill comes out of committee.*

2. *After you have had a success in committee, start recruiting legislative allies outside the committee. Leadership support is especially valuable.*

3. *Beware of losing your bill between the committee and the floor. Be alert to sneak attacks and be ready to counter them.*

4. *New issues, perennial issues, and uncontroversial technical issues all require different lobbying strategies and tactics.*

5. *Before you begin lobbying, analyze who can be expected to oppose you, and why. The positions of the governor and the legislative leadership are especially important.*

6. *Set priorities. Contact key legislators first.*

7. *A lobbyist cannot be shy. You must seek out and approach the legislators.*

8. *Tailor your approach to the interests and personalities of individual legislators.*

9. *There are two legislative chambers in every state except Nebraska. Unless you are in Nebraska, then, do not forget about monitoring one chamber while lobbying the other.*

10. *Many important decisions are made in party caucuses. If the caucuses are open to you, be there; if they are not open, ask legislative allies to keep you informed.*

☆ **11** ☆

Floor Debate

"Mr. Speaker, members of the Assembly . . ."

This is your moment of truth. Your bill has reached the august chamber of the state Assembly. The moment is a solemn one—or so it seems until the debate is interrupted by a tumultuous standing ovation for the majority leader's flashy sport jacket.

Any remaining illusions we may have cherished about the seriousness with which legislators would treat debates were dispelled when we heard muffled cries of "Vote, vote, vote" from a rambunctious group of unofficial time-keepers in the back rows of the House chamber whenever a debate went over the five minute mark. With three weeks left in the session, one member paged through the bills on this desk, rose during an uneventful debate and proclaimed, "Mr. Speaker, I've read over all the bills that are coming up in the next few weeks and none of them are worth looking at. I move that we adjourn right now so we don't waste the entire session." To the further astonishment of many in the house, his motion was promptly seconded.

These and other antics prompt the question most frequently asked by new observers of the legislative process: Does floor debate actually influence legislators and the outcome of legislation? On controversial issues, most legislators know how they will vote before the floor debate begins. Lobbyists have been bombarding them with specially prepared information, various interest groups from their districts have made their positions known, and individual constituents have written or called to voice their opinions.

Having already made up their minds, many legislators leave the chamber during debate to attend to more pressing matters, such as reading newspapers or eating and drinking. Unless the bill is especially controversial or a television camera is on, many of those who remain in the chamber are catching up on sleep or paperwork.

At times, you cannot blame the legislators for seeking escape. What legislative speakers have to say is not always worth listening to. On certain issues everyone wants to have his or her statement on the record, regardless of whether anything new is added; repetition becomes the order of the day. Certain members are notorious for rambling on for 10 or 15 minutes on the most trivial of subjects. As soon as they stand up to speak, the chamber empties.

Unfortunately, legislators often extend this bored impatience toward floor debate on any issue. There are, of course, a few legislators who insist on listening to the debate before they decide how to vote. This seems like a sensible approach, but it is not always the best way to make an intelligent decision. During debate, legislators have no real opportunity to verify the facts (usually provided by lobbyists) thrown casually about the chamber. Emotion, not logic, often reigns supreme.

Despite all its flaws, floor debate can be important, particularly if your bill has not aroused much controversy. In that case, many legislators may hear of the bill for the first time when it reaches the floor; they will pay closer attention to the debate. The less advance controversy generated by a bill, the larger and more crucial the bloc of uncommitted votes becomes, and the more significant the floor debate becomes, because legislators have simply not thought much about the issue beforehand.

A lobbyist, however, must always think about the issue before the debate. Derisive comments about the quality of debate are little comfort when your bill is unexpectedly defeated on the floor.

PREPARING FOR FLOOR DEBATE

Strategy sessions. As the date for floor debate on your bill draws near, strategy sessions should be held with the principal supporters — especially the representative or senator who will introduce the bill — and other legislators who plan to provide backup support. Any new information on the issue — revised studies, new findings, new recommendations, position reassessments, warnings of harmful amendments — should be quickly passed on to your supporters. Most of the time, you will have little advance warning of exactly when your bill will come to a vote. You should begin preparations as soon as you get the slightest indication that your bill is about to come to the floor. To obtain this information, rely especially on the chairperson or members and staff of the committee that reported the bill.

At your strategy sessions, specific tactics should be discussed: How should the bill be introduced, what points should be emphasized, what can be expected from the opposition? You will not always feel that you have time to bring your supporters together for meetings like these, but if your opponents are strong, you should make the time. They will.

Anticipating the debate. If you expect trouble on the floor when your bill comes up for debate, line up additional supporters beforehand who will be there to rush to your assistance and speak for your bill if needed. These "safety margin" legislators can be approached by you or by the chief sponsor. If the debate runs smoothly, these reinforcements may not have to be called into action, but it is reassuring to know that help is waiting in the wings.

It is extremely important that your sponsors familiarize

themselves with any arguments the opposing side may throw at them during debate. Be sure your supporters have facts and figures literally *at their fingertips* to refute these arguments. Data filed in your office will do little good during the debate.

Offer to help the legislator introducing your bill or your other slated supporters prepare for the debate. A legislator trying to keep the attention of his or her colleagues may have a task equivalent to teaching Shakespeare to high-school students, so he or she must be knowledgeable and articulate

If the legislator bringing your bill to the floor has political liabilities damaging to your chances, you may need to employ a pinch-hitter. The chief proponent of the Connecticut bottle bill in 1976 was a young Republican who was not a member of either the environment committee, which had reported out the bill, or the dominant Democratic party. Since the Democrats would probably have rejected *any* bill proposed by a Republican, we pressed a Democratic member of the environment committee into service as the introducer. He had never heard of the issue before the start of the session, but after a few weeks of briefing by our lobbyist, the committee staff, and legislative research personnel, he was transformed into a full-fledged expert and presented a credible and effective argument in floor debate.

Amendments. During the strategy sessions, it is important to consider possible amendment—both for you and against you. If you are lucky, you may hear of your opponent's plans to try to amend your bill two or three days before the floor debate, but usually you hear about these little surprises only a few hours before your bill hits the floor. Check with the clerk's office; if there are any new amendments, get copies, study them carefully, and prepare your arguments against them.

In some states, amendments can be introduced on the floor without prior registration. The only way to find out about these amendments is to keep in close touch with your contacts in the legislature and to spend plenty of time at the capitol, engaging legislators and lobbyists in conversation to elicit bits and pieces of information.

Your own ammunition. You too can have amendments ready to defuse legislation you oppose. One minority leader in Connecticut has been known to offer more than 20 amendments to bills particularly offensive to him. Many legislators expect these prolonged performances by the minority. These amendments, though they might actually be constructive alterations, are chiefly symbolic and are usually defeated, unless sides are evenly matched or the issue cuts across party lines.

Citizen groups, like minority parties, can work to delete vital sections with amendments, alter the intent of legislation, or push the effective date of a bill off into the 21st century. Naturally, you have to convince legislators to offer these drastic amendments. Unless they are already vitally concerned about the issue, they are not likely to make the effort if you cannot convince them that certain bills will directly hurt the public.

You may be fortunate to have the opportunity to *add* something constructive to a proposed bill. If you plan to amend a bill backed by the majority party, make sure that the amendment is introduced by an influential majority member or that the nonpartisan nature of the suggested change is fully explained.

Amendments can also be a handy way of introducing an issue that would otherwise not reach the floor. Such maneuvers, used often by party leaders, usually occur late in legislative sessions, when committee deadlines have passed and offering an amendment is the only way to bring a new issue to the floor. Officially, there has to be some connection between the bill and the amendment attached to it, but a direct relationship is often difficult to perceive.

The Nature of the Debate

Most bills that come before a legislature are not particularly controversial. They are usually introduced without fanfare, a few comments are made, some questions are asked, and then the votes follow party, geographical, or ideological lines. Most of the work has already been done behind the scenes by the chief proponents and interested lobbyists. Their task now is to gently guide their legislation through by convincing the members that this is a "good bill" that will not rock the boat but will alleviate a particular problem or assist a deserving group of people. In many cases, *to trumpet a bill as a "landmark effort" is to beg for defeat.* It is for that very reason that you should try to direct as much attention as possible to any bill you are fighting. When you are opposing a measure, the more controversy the better.

Often the debate will not even touch upon a bill's substantive issues. Legislators on the floor will concentrate instead on proposing and fighting a multitude of complex parliamentary maneuvers employed to block legislation. Leaders and other influential legislators have many opportunities to dispose of unwanted legislation long before it reaches the floor, but if a bill has managed to survive to this point a quick referral or rapid recommittal to committee is an effective way to dump it without facing up to its merits.

While it is helpful to recognize that legislators have limitations and that debates are not models of textbooks civics, do not be deluded into complete cynicism about the worth of floor debate.

Remember: Legislators usually have very little time to research or even read most of the bills that reach the floor for consideration each day. Many of these bills could be significant, but they simply have not received the advance publicity or all-out lobbying efforts that grace a few issues each session.

The presentation and the way your sponsors handle any unexpected emergencies will have a great bearing on the final outcome, not necessarily through the logic of their remarks, but through their ability to control the tone of the debate. Your strategy sessions in advance of the debate and your ability to find out what is happening in caucus will determine how effectively your supporters control the debate.

WATCHING THE ACTION: THE LOBBYIST'S ROLE

During the late stages of the legislative session, we found ourselves spending large chunks of time in the balcony galleries that surrounded the legislature's chambers. As we waited for our legislation to make its debut on the floor, we listened to the other floor debates for the insights they offered into the character of the Assembly and its members. We sometimes picked up ideas on more effective ways to persuade certain legislators. We often saw a different side to one of our supporters, which told us whether we could fully depend upon him or her to push our issues. One legislative leader told us several times that he supported particular bills and even endorsed them publicly, but when it came time for him to use his influence to get a bill out of committee or to speak in behalf of a bill in caucus, he was usually silent. His version of leadership was not ours.

When our bills came to the floor, we followed the debates closely from the galleries. Matters *seemed* completely out of our control, but our job was not yet over. Of course, we could not participate in the debate. It is considered particularly bad form to signal legislators from the gallery with sign language or cue cards. Sometimes a legislator would motion to meet us off the floor to ask a question or fill us in on behind-the-scenes politicking. But during the debate, we were usually forced to sit back and silently cultivate ulcers. (A legislator can ask the speaker to permit nonlegislators on the floor during a session, but this may bring accusations that "lobbyists are running everything.")

The rhythm of the debate is the key factor in judging when to stand firm and when to compromise. If the bill arouses any controversy, people on both sides of the issue will speak on it. Strong, forceful speakers with particularly persuasive arguments, or several advocates speaking consecutively, can change the outcome of a debate.

The sponsor and other legislators supporting your bill should be present to follow the full flow of the debate. If your side appears to be losing ground, it may be safer to move to pass over the matter temporarily, giving you time to work out a compromise amendment designed to save the bill from total loss.

The danger, naturally, is in compromising when your side actually has the votes to pass your version.

AFTER THE DEBATE

Reconsiderations. By the time your vote is tallied, you will probably feel totally drained. If your bill has passed, congratulations. If not, before collapsing, pause a moment to scan the final vote.

If the vote is extremely close—less than a four- or five-vote margin—look over the tally sheet, which can usually be obtained from the clerk after the votes are registered. Look for legislators you might persuade to reconsider their votes. In some states, a motion to reconsider—to bring a bill back to the floor for another vote—can only be made by a legislator who voted on the *winning* side of the issue. Beware of time limitations too. In Connecticut, motions to reconsider must be made within a day after the initial vote was counted.

If you plan to try for reconsideration, scour the voting sheet for friendly legislators who might change their position with a little coaxing or who might have misunderstood a complicated vote. Contact these prospects as soon as you can. Call them off the floor if necessary, and emphasize again the importance of your issue. All you need is one commitment to reconsider, but that is easier said than done. If you *are* able to win over one misguided soul, quickly alert other legislators who might change their votes that a motion to reconsider will be made.

Word of any reconsideration move usually spreads rapidly through the legislative grapevine. Remember: Reconsideration is a long shot at best. The chamber must first vote to allow a reconsideration—no easy achievement. Many legislators vote against *all* reconsiderations on the principle that all votes should be final. If the motion to reconsider passes, another vote is then taken on the bill itself. Successful reconsiderations are rare and are usually initiated by the governor, the leadership, or others who have the power to force legislators to change their positions.

Referrals. If your bill is not defeated on the floor but is referred back to a committee, where it is expected to wither and die, you need not give up. If referral came because a floor amendment tacked a financing provision on your bill, your job is indeed difficult. Tacking on unnecessary state funding to a bill otherwise having no cost is a sure-fire way to defeat the legislation. It also avoids the incriminating evidence that a recorded vote on the bill itself would leave behind. Appeal to the legislators' sense of justice by asking why the bill was sent to the committee. This is the time to be the righteous public interest martyr. "Is it the committee's job to silently block the legislation?" "Is this how the legislative process really works, with sleight of hand behind closed doors and last-minute betrayals?" Ask that the bill be immediately approved by the committee and sent back to the floor—where it should have stayed in the first place and where a vote on the merits, including any attached costs, can be taken. (These actions, of course, can only be taken if referral occurs within the deadline for a committee to report bills or within the time limit for petitioning. If it occurs beyond these deadlines, there may be no way to resurrect the bill.)

Do not forget the press. Whether you win or lose the vote, let the press—especially members of the capitol press corps—know your reactions to it. If you have worked hard for a piece of legislation and won, you deserve the credit; if you have lost, the public ought to know what defeated the measure and what you plan to do next. Prepare press statements ahead of time for release when you know the outcome.

SUMMARY

1. With your legislative allies, plan your strategy for the floor debate well in advance.

2. Anticipate problems before the debate, and be ready to counter.

3. Be prepared for possible amendments offered by the opposition, and have your own amendments ready to disarm legislation you oppose.

4. Remember that on many issues, legislators have decided how to vote before the floor debate begins.

5. Concentrate on convincing the uncommitted legislators.

6. The debate is most important for those bills that have not attracted much attention beforehand.

7. When you are working for *a bill, try to avoid controversy; when you are working* against *a bill, try to stimulate debate.*

8. Legislators usually have little time to read and research most bills; frame your debate strategy with this in mind.

9. Attempt to have your supporters control the debate.

10. If you lose a close vote, try to have the matter "reconsidered." Do not forget that your opponents can do the same.

11. Let the press and the public know your reactions to the decision on your bill.

☆ **12** ☆

After the Session

On a warm Saturday morning in July we prepare to enjoy one of the pleasures of a weekend in the office—a leisurely reading of the local paper. We get as far as the headline on page 5: GOVERNOR VETOES BILL CREATING WEST ROCK PARK.

Long hours of work, scores of phone calls, painstaking months at the legislature cajoling and reasoning—all down the drain.

The veto is the best illustration of the rule that a good lobbyist cannot stop working when the legislature does. The legislative process continues to operate and you must too.

IF YOUR LEGISLATION PASSES

Stop for a second to pat yourself and your co-workers on the back. Thank (preferably with personal phone calls) those who helped you pass your legislation. All of them, especially the politicians, like to be acknowledged and remembered. You will need their help in the future. But you are allowed only a brief pause for self-congratulations. You must make sure your bill, so close to being law, fulfils its promise.

On the Governor's Desk

Once your bill passes the legislature, work to get the governor to sign the bill (except in North Carolina, where the

175

governor has no veto power). In lobbying for the bill you may have tried to get the governor's support. If the governor is already committed to the bill, especially publicly, it is likely the bill will be signed—but examine the political scene; commitments can change rapidly.

If you are not sure how the governor stands, talk to the governor's aides. Your relationship with the governor and the staff will tell you whether you can trust their comments. But even if the governor says he or she is for the bill it does not hurt to provide reinforcement. Have groups and citizens who support the bill write letters and telegrams and make telephone calls, urging the governor to sign it. It is better to make this effort than to find that your bill has been unexpectedly vetoed.

If the governor is unsure about signing the bill, or is opposed to it, it is time for you to go back to work, usually in public. You have the same tactics available as when you lobbied in the legislature—press releases, letters, phone calls. You have to make the signing of the bill a political issue. This is especially important when you know the governor is hostile. Make it clear that the governor will be solely responsible for that simple pen stroke of veto.

On one bill, we gathered more than 17,000 petition signatures, which we handed over to the governor's office as television cameras whirred. Despite his former oppostion, the governor signed our bill.

Focus your energy. You may not want to attract media attention to every bill awaiting the governor's signature. If you believe the governor is likely to sign the bill, and there is no opposition power threatening to outflank you, there is no need to publicize the signing. That is especially true when implications of the bill are controversial but did not receive much public attention. Publicity about the bill would only attract the attention of those inclined to oppose it, whom you may have already outmaneuvered.

CCAG did not mount a public campaign to have the governor sign a bill to establish a nuclear power evaluation council because we believed the governor was already inclined to support the bill. Given a series of recent, much-publicized nuclear power accidents in Connecticut, signing the bill would let her say she was doing something about a serious problem. There was no need to turn the signing of a useful bill into a debate on nuclear power.

The Governor Signs the Bill: No Rest for the Weary

Once the governor has signed the bill, you think you have won and jubilant victory celebrations can begin. Wrong again. First, you have to make sure people hear about the new law's benefits and how *you* made them possible. Letters to the editor from prominent groups or citizens extolling your victory can enhance the impact of your future efforts and increase public awareness of the new law.

Second, and most important, *you must monitor what happens to the law.* There are many ways for a law to be rendered useless or actually harmful to the citizens you sought to aid. The time to start worrying about this is *before* the bill passes. You can anticipate trouble and prepare for it, rather than reacting hurriedly to emergencies.

Whose Bailiwick?

Most legislation designates a state agency to draft detailed regulations implementing it. Which agency is designated can be critical in determining whether the law is gutted by bureaucratic scheming or given real meaning through vigorous enforcement. CCAG struggled for more than a year over a simple set of regulations to enforce a law permitting pharmacists to post prescription drug prices. The General Assembly had designated the Pharmacy Commission, over our opposition, to draft the regulations. Like most professional boards, the commission was composed entirely of the more traditional members of the pharmacy profession. (Because of CCAG's efforts, public members have since been appointed to the commission.) Had the Department of Consumer Protection been responsible for drafting the regulations, a lot of our problems could have been avoided. In working for a bill, aim to have it designate the most sympathetic agency to draft regulations.

Legislative History: Anticipating Reconstructionists

Everything said about a bill during its legislative journey is part of its "legislative history." Legislative history includes committee reports, transcripts of committee hearings, and floor debates. If your state keeps such written records, they can be important tools for you. If there are ever any questions about the intent of a law or the interpretation of an ambiguous phrase, the law's legislative history will be examined to find the answer. Therefore it is vital that the legislative history be one that will support *your* intent in having your bill passed. On the other hand, for a bill inimical to the public interest, it may be equally important to mount a last-ditch effort to include language weakening the effect of the bad measure.

The most important part of the legislative history is the committee report on the bill. Ask your allies on the committee to insert language in the committee report to clarify any ambiguities about critical aspects of the bill. If there is no committee report or if you do not get the language you want in the report, the next best thing is to have the chairperson of the committee (or whoever is handling the bill on the floor) make the statements you want when explaining the bill on the floor. This at least puts these remarks on record in the official transcript. From the time the bill is introduced in committee until it is passed, there are many other opportunities for recorded discussion of what the bill means or is intended to do. All of these are part of the legislative history.

Regulatory Games

Once your bill (with its carefully guided legislative history) is signed, it is *regulation time*. You will need to learn the diverse ways that regulatory agencies can play with your bill, which now seems so solidly and safely entrenched as law. Do not expect your lobbying efforts to have much real success for the public you serve if you do not become adept at these regulatory exercises.

Remember that your opponents, whether industry lobbyists or ideological rivals, will continue their efforts to defeat you, even after you have won in the legislature and on the governor's desk. Your rivals may have access to the regulatory agency staff responsible for drafting the regulations for your new law. The agency itself may have been your primary opponent. You can expect to find any opposition to your bill mirrored in the writing of regulations. Be on the alert for moves to destroy the effectiveness of your bill.

CCAG's jousting with the State Pharmacy Commission serves as a good example of this game. The 1973 legislature had decided neither to mandate the posting nor to permit the advertising of prescription drug prices, but simply to *allow* pharmacy owners to *voluntarily* post their prescription prices. The legislature gave the responsibility for drafting the regulations to the industry-controlled Pharmacy Commission. The pharmacy industry had doggedly fought all legislative attempts to give consumers more price information.

The commission's regulations required that, once a store decided to post prices, it had to post the prices of the hundred drugs most frequently prescribed *by that particular pharmacy.* CCAG had recommended that the stores post the prices of the hundred drugs most commonly prescribed *in the state.* The regulations meant that even if pharmacists went to the trouble to calculate their sales patterns and post their prices, there still would be no way for consumers to compare prices, since the drugs posted would vary from one pharmacy to another. Consumers would still lack the information needed to comparison shop.

The Pharmacy Commission also rejected our suggestion that pharmacists be permitted to provide smaller copies of the wall poster so that consumers could take the price information with them and not have to stand embarrassed in the store, laboriously copying the information.

The legislature had specifically indicated its intent to "assist the public in making informed purchasing decisions" and ensure "the availability of factual information" about prescription prices, but the commission was more interested in protecting pharmacists than consumers.

The commission's hard-line position backfired. CCAG convinced legislators that the regulations made the law a sham and that the only solution was to *allow* advertising and *require* posting.

The delay game. This runaround is characterized by indifference, unresponsiveness, and continuous foot-dragging by the regulatory agency, with the result that no regulations are implemented to enforce the law. CCAG once encountered this example carried to its extreme.

In 1972, the Connecticut legislature passed the Environmental Policy Act, requiring environmental impact statements for state construction projects. The bill was vetoed by the governor, who then issued an executive ordering requiring impact statements. The order was never enforced. In 1973 the legislature passed another Environmental Policy Act, to take effect two years later, in February 1975. The State Department of Environmental Protection was given those two years to draft regulations. Two years came and went. The agency held hearings but issued no regulations. The attorney general said the law was "too vague" and had "technical problems," yet no corrective legislation was proposed.

We were considering going to court over the lack of regulations when the governor proposed postponing the law's effective date another 14 months. With a strong lobbying effort we were able to stop the postponement, but the legislature revoked the Department of Environmental Protection's authority to issue regulations to implement the law. Now each regulatory agency, none of them very sensitive to environmental problems, could come up with its own self-serving procedures for submitting environmental impact statements in its issue area.

In 1972, we won a major environmental victory, only to see it delayed by stalling. Three years later we had to fight the same battle all over again simply to keep a weakened version of the law on the books.

Throwing away the rule book. This game is even harder to deal with than the problem of an agency refusing to draft regulations. Here the agency drafts regulations, even good ones, and then ignores the regulations and the law. The law's intentions are good, the agency claims, but either the law is "unworkable" or there is "insufficient staff for adequate enforcement." The word, of course, soon spreads to those business interests that are supposed to be regulated that the enforcing agency has no intention of doing anything about the law.

Unit pricing laws, for example, are widely unenforced. In Connecticut and other states, these laws require that the price *per unit* (per pound, ounce, quart, dozen, and so forth) of a product be placed on a shelf label next to the total price, to enable shoppers to easily compare prices of similar products in different package sizes.

In a survey by our research offshoot, the Connecticut Citizen Research Group, almost 50 percent of the more than 1,300 items surveyed lacked unit price labels or had labels that were out of date, unreadable, or in the wrong location. Half the violations were for a total absence of a unit price sticker. Stores did not even try to comply with the law, because no one made them do so.

The definition game. CCAG was overjoyed when it helped pass an amendment requiring a certain percentage of transportation funds to be spent for mass transportation. This apparent victory for mass transit depends heavily on how "mass transportation" is defined. The State Department of Transportation thought that an excellent example of mass transportation was a $4.5 million minitrain to carry people between the parking lot and terminal at the state's main airport. Meanwhile the state's inadequate bus and rail systems were steadily deteriorating. Only the governor, his transportation officials, and the builder (Ford Motor Company) wanted the "People Mover," which was nicknamed "Tommie's Trolley" in honor of Governor Thomas J. Meskill. We got the state legislature to formally reject the project and remove it from the mass transportation bond authorization bill, but the Department of Transportation found the funds elsewhere.

Economics triumphed in the end. Today the "People Mover" lies idle, shut down by the governor who thought it was a waste of money. It gathers dust as a monument to the definition game.

The appointments game. You have worked hard to pass a bill creating a commission to study alternatives to nuclear power. You are elated by your success—until the governor announces the members appointed to the commission: five utility executives, one former state legislator known for pronuclear views, and a "public representative" who knows nothing about energy issues.

The best legislation can be rendered meaningless with lackluster appointments. On the other hand, the appointment of an aggressive, innovative advocate for the real needs of citizens can turn an agency that has been cozying up to special interests into an effective defender of the consumer.

If you are working on legislation that creates appointive positions, be careful to build in measures to ensure that appointees are not captives of special political interests.

Regulation writing. Earlier we stressed the importance of drawing up your own draft of a bill before you begin lobbying. It is also wise to draw up your own draft of regulations to implement your bill. Give your model regulations to the appropriate agency before it issues its own; this is one way to try to forestall ineffective regulations.

Most states have some administrative procedure for citizens to petition for the adoption of agency regulations. Get to know the procedure in your state. If the agency is dragging its feet, submit your own regulations for approval. If you know the agency is working on its own regulations, give the most sympathetic persons involved in writing the regulations a copy of your version. Even if you have no sympathetic persons to give your draft to, give it to the agency staff anyway. It will let them know you are monitoring their actions.

Of course, you should participate in any hearings on the regulations. Many of the comments made earlier about committee hearings also apply to agency hearings.

Changing the Handwriting on the Wall

What happens if the regulations still do not turn out the way you want?

Again, almost every state has some procedure for appealing decisions of administrative agencies, including regulations they develop. Many states have legislative committees that review agency regulations to see if the legislature's intent is carried out.

If the legislative review committee will not act, you can challenge the regulations in court on the grounds that they subvert the intent of the legislature, as expressed in the legislative history.

Before you get to that point, though, try to get the agency to enforce the regulations properly. Use informal contacts with agency personnel to find out what is being done and to communicate your opinions. Keep in touch with administrators and key legislators to discuss enforcement. Lobby agency staff the way you do legislators. Even though they are not elected, they are public servants.

CCAG has received several tips about agency subversion

of the public interest from friendly agency staffers who were disgruntled about a decision. They have turned to us because things are going badly inside the agency. Friendly staffers can provide you with documents that you otherwise would not know about or would have difficulty obtaining. It is often difficult for public interest lobbyists to establish this close relationship with agency staffers because of high turnover on both sides. Nevertheless, it is essential to keep up relationships and contacts, and to avoid having all your dealings with an agency sound like major investigations.

While being friendly with your agency contacts is important, you must feel free to criticize an agency when it makes an improper decision. Publicity is often the most effective tool you can use to deal with a state agency. Many state agencies operate almost invisibly; even citizens who pride themselves on being politically active seldom know the name of their state transportation commissioner or health commissioner.

A survey showing that an agency is failing to enforce a consumer protection law can attract publicity and bring tremendous public and legislative pressure to bear on the agency.

If you have access to legal counsel, other formidable tactics can be brought into play. For instance, through a *mandamus* action, you can appeal to a state court to require the commissioner of an agency, or even the governor, to enforce a law. Simply the threat of doing this can generate much attention and possibly get an agency moving. If the content of existing regulations is insufficient in specific ways, you may also be able to initiate a *rulemaking procedure.* Under administrative regulations in many states, citizens can call upon an agency to add and delete regulations, so long as the change lies within the agency's statutory authority.

For more details on dealing with state agencies, read *Getting Action: How to Petition State Government* by Carl Oshiro and Harry Snyder (Consumers Union, 1980).

Legislative oversight. Legislators typically take very little interest in scrutinizing executive agencies' enforcement of laws. Yet individual legislators and committees have this oversight authority, and you should press them to exercise it. You can thus achieve another forum for your views and bring pressure upon an agency from another angle.

CCAG has long argued that one of the most important roles of state legislatures is to monitor the performance of executive agencies. The natural tendency of legislators not to stir up trouble for the agencies they have to work with (especially when the legislature is controlled by the same party controlling the state administration) is the most frequent obstacle. In many states, a lack of sufficient legislative staff also discourages legislators from delving very deeply.

The legislators most likely to be interested in agency misconduct are those who originally introduced the legislation being mangled. Their pride and their desire to see results from their legislation, even if only to impress the folks back home, can work to your benefit. Search out those legislators with reputations for independent action. Present your evidence of agency ineffectiveness; you might find a champion.

If you successfully kick off an oversight hearing, be prepared to feed detailed information to the legislators involved and, where possible, to testify yourself. If you have convinced legislators to challenge an agency, you have a responsibility to assist that legislator.

Refine your legislation. No bill is perfect—even yours. Be prepared to point out problems with your legislation so that corrective action can be taken in a subsequent session of the legislature. If you do not do it, your opponents will.

Build on Success

If you succeed in passing a bill this year that accomplishes part of your goal, think of what action naturally follows and work to get that legislation through next year. If you get through a bill mandating the posting of prescription drug prices, then perhaps next year you should push a bill permitting pharmacists to advertise the prescription drug prices. Or, you may want to advocate a bill permitting pharmacists to substitute lower-priced generic drugs for higher-priced brand-name drugs. But do not expect to move too fast. Legislators usually want to change things one step at a time.

IF A BAD BILL PASSES

This chapter deals mostly with what to do if your bill passes. What happens if an opponent's bill passes?

Obviously, you want to stop it as soon as you can. The first possible place is the governor's desk.

The governor's veto power, to be feared when your bill passes, can be a last reprieve when a bad bill passes. One of the best ways to defeat a bill is to create as much controversy about it as you can. Raise uncertainties about the issues underlying the bill, referring to all that is sacrosanct within the American political system. The bill may "cost too much," "violate local autonomy," "sell the consumer down the drain," or be a "a giveaway to special interests." Emphasize publicly that if the governor signs the bill, she or he could be violating one or more of these principles.

If you cannot get a veto, there is always next year or the year after to work for repeal of bad legislation. Keep the problems of the bill in the public eye. Make sure the legislators and special interests who worked against you are given wide coverage for their "bad" vote and lobbying.

IF YOUR LEGISLATION FAILS

Legislation you advocate may fail the first time around. If the issue were an easy one to win, then you would probably not be working on it. Pushing resolutions supporting apple pie or motherhood is not your job. Never forget that you may "lose" more often than you win. That does not mean that you should expect defeat or should not fight hard to win, but do not begin lobbying with illusions of instant success.

If your bill is defeated, do not spend your time moping. That temporary setback should be the time for starting on your next project or beginning your plans for the next legislative session. Don't mourn, organize.

What Went Wrong

The first part of making any new plans for legislation is a careful analysis of what went wrong. Not enough research? Poor press work? Supporters not organized? Wrong approaches to legislative leadership?

This is the time to review all the pointers that have been suggested previously for what goes into a successful effort. No one—not you, not CCAG, not even the highest-paid corporate lobbyist—does everything exactly right. Talk to your supporters, your friends in the press, legislators with whom you worked—even your opponents—about what happened. They all have slightly different perspectives and can point out problems from their various vantage points.

Do not engage in pointless breast-beating over a failure. Legislation is sometimes lost for reasons you have very little control over: budget crises, personality conflicts, or internal political maneuvers.

The point is to see what happened, learn from any mistakes, avoid discouragement, and start working immediately on future plans.

In making these plans, there are several things to remember:

Do not expect overnight victories. Citizen lobbyists usually work on tough issues and have to come back time after time to get legislation passed. It took CCAG four years to pass the posting of prescription drug prices. It took us four years to get legislation ensuring that consumers would no longer pay for most advertising by utility companies. It took many years to pass the bottle bill.

On the other hand, persistence does not mean mulelike stubbornness. Reexamine your approach to the problem. Maybe you need a different bill. Maybe there would be a better forum for presenting the issue. Perhaps an administrative agency could handle the problem better than the legislature. Be persistent, but be adaptable.

Compromise. If you are tenacious and realize that winning on an issue takes time, then you will be prepared to accept halfway measures on occasion. In 1973 CCAG pushed for legislation to permit the advertising and require the posting of prescription drug prices. The counteroffer was to allow the advertising but to make the posting of prices voluntary. But we took it. When our survey showed that few pharmacists voluntarily posted prices, we had hard evidence to show that the original bill was not working and that we needed the "whole loaf." In the next legislative session, both prescription drug bills passed. Our first measure established the principle that consumers had a right to this information; our second and third measures gave them the means to acquire it.

There is a difference between accepting a meaningful compromise that accomplishes a reform and something that simply gives the illusion of progress. Compromise legislation that provides nothing for you to build on is a dead end. Make sure that any compromise you accept at least begins to address the problem.

Losing in the Public Interest

CCAG fought the state pharmacy association tooth and nail on the issues of drug price advertising and posting, but the association later turned out to be our strongest ally in the fight to permit pharmacists to substitute lower-priced generic drugs for brand-name drugs. There may be adversaries you will rarely want to deal with again, but as a general rule, do not engage in invective. If you do, it may be impossible to ever work with your opponents on other issues.

This is not to say that you should never publicly criticize an opponent. Public interest lobbyists have to. It is good to let your opponents know that they can expect to be held accountable for their actions. You will gain greater respect for your efforts.

If your group handles a variety of issues, you will have to get accustomed to hearing disagreement on some issues from people who support you on others. Forget about achieving unanimity and keep the doors open to temporary alliances.

The Thrill of Victory

One of the main lessons of public interest advocacy is how slowly the legislative process moves. Victory comes on very few issues. It is easy for your supporters, your co-workers, and even you to get discouraged at the snail's pace and say, "I've had it. We're not getting anywhere."

That is why upbeat thinking is so critical for citizen lobbyists and citizen groups. Morale is valuable currency for people dedicated to serving the public interest rather than to lining their own pockets. Emphasize your successes. Every lobbying effort has some successes—even if it did not pass a single bill. Perhaps one of your bills got further than it ever had before. Perhaps you educated a large number of legislators on a particular issue. Perhaps you received a tremendous outpouring of public support at a hearing. Perhaps you received a favorable editorial or two. These are all steps to eventual success. Stress these positive results to your staff and your supporters and emphasize the need to build upon them. This reinforcement can keep an organization from going sour from frustration.

SUMMARY

1. The passage of your legislation is not the end of your job. The governor's signature, agency regulations, appointments, and enforcement all require continued attention.

2. Do not assume the governor will sign your bill. Be prepared to challenge a potential veto.

3. *The legislative history of a bill may determine just how much your bill can accomplish. Be sure that the record supports your intent.*

4. *Regulations can make or break a bill. The legislation should be designed to go to the most supportive agency, and you must participate in and monitor the drafting process.*

5. *Regulatory games can include outright subversion of the intent of your bill, delay, failure to enforce adequate regulations, misleading definitions, and poor appointments.*

6. *Ultimately, you have recourse against regulatory games in the legislature or the courts.*

7. *If a bad bill passes, a gubernatorial veto or eventual repeal are your options.*

8. *Remember that public interest victories come slowly and only after great effort. Do not be discouraged by failure; learn from it. Getting halfway to your goal in one legislative session means you start out that much further along your road in the next session.*

☆ 13 ☆

Conclusion: Citizens for Change

Much has changed at state capitols since the days when legislation received little public scrutiny and legislators were able to vote with no one knowing how they voted. It is much more difficult now for the scene with the insurance lobbyist described at the beginning of this book to take place.

State legislatures have changed and continue to change—for the better. Reapportionment spurred by the U.S. Supreme Court's one-man one-vote ruling has made them more representative. The days when a lawmaker representing a few people and many cows had the same weight as a legislator representing a densely populated urban area are gone forever.

State legislatures—just like Congress—are attempting to reassert their function as coequal branches with the more powerful executives. The general trend is toward annual and longer sessions, a streamlining of procedures to make for greater efficiency, higher salaries, a beefing-up of professional staff to provide independent information, and a greater emphasis on overseeing executive implementation of legislative programs.

Most important, state legislatures are becoming more open and accessible to the public—and more accountable. Thirty states now require committee hearings to be open, although this is not always true for executive or voting sessions. A roll call is now required for many floor votes. The roll call vote, however, as we have seen, does not mean that a legislator will vote intelligently or even know what he or she is voting on. Many legislators still rush in at the last minute looking to see how party colleagues are voting and then follow suit, but at least they are on record and must answer for their votes if challenged.

Bills, roll call votes, and transcripts of hearings and floor debates should be accessible to the public. Computers and electronic roll call machines contribute to their accessibility. Once bills and procedural actions have been logged in a computer, it is less likely that bills can get "lost" as they once did.

Many legislators have a narrow interest—a particular issue, a bill strictly for home consumption, or one backed by a special interest—and spend most of their time pursuing it. That, plus carrying out the daily constituent chores and earning a living, leaves little time for learning anything about all the issues considered in the legislature.

In Connecticut, only the leadership and the committee chairpersons have personal staff. The rank and file must rely on an overworked pool of researchers and secretaries. Legislators who have an unpaid intern or volunteer to help them out are way ahead of their colleagues.

Hundreds of bills reach the floor for final action in the last weeks of the session, without legislators having anywhere near enough time to read them. Surely the public interest is not served by a process that depends more on luck than on good planning and management.

Institutional limitations make state legislatures more susceptible to the influence of special interest lobbyists because most legislators do not have the resources and time to investigate the other side.

Most legislatures do not even have the time or staff to investigate what goes on across town in the state's executive agencies. The legislature may pass good legislation, but who monitors the implementation of the law? More often than not, no one.

And who monitors the legislature? Again, the answer is frequently "no one," for the simple reason that the necessary information is too often unavailable. Cracks are spreading, however, in the walls of secrecy surrounding most legislatures. Freedom-of-information laws, tougher standards of ethics, fuller disclosure of financial interests, stricter regulation of lobbyists, and laws requiring open meetings have started to be passed due to citizen pressure. Continued pressure can further the process.

Another step that would dramatically increase citizen participation in government is the enactment of a constitutional amendment in all 50 states creating an initiative and referendum process. Already established in 23 states, this process gives *citizens* the power to pass laws directly. The initiative is open government in its simplest and purest form.

The present system makes citizens subservient to their legislators and leaves the legislature subservient to any executive who chooses to dominate it. Connecticut citizens would be horrified if they could observe the General Assembly for a week and see the conditions under which members have to work.

Many legislatures should be full-time, with expert staff and adequate facilities. The cost would be saved many times over by wise decisions. But the public remains skeptical— justifiably —about the need to spend money for improving government when its performance has disappointed and disillusioned so many. A change to a full-time legislature will have to await an aroused public, involved in the legislative process and convinced that their representatives are accountable to them. Only then will it willingly put up dollars for an effective legislative branch.

The reforms of the past decade have made state capitols potentially fertile ground for citizen action. Whether state capitols remain shrouded in mystery or are opened to the bright glare of public attention depends largely on you, the citizen lobbyist.

Appendix: Resources

DIRECTORY OF
PUBLIC INTEREST RESEARCH GROUPS

Public Interest Research Groups (PIRGs) are nonprofit nonpartisan research and education organizations that are directed and voluntarily funded by students. A full-time professional staff of attorneys, scientists, writers, and organizers assist the students. PIRGs work on consumer, environment, energy, and government-reform projects.

California PIRG (CalPIRG)
6 Shattuck Sq., room 11
Berkeley, California 94704
(415) 642-9952
contact: Jerry Skommer

Colorado PIRG (CoPIRG)
520 York St.
Denver, CO 80206
(303) 355-1861
contact: Thomas Wathen,
    director

Connecticut PIRG (ConnPIRG)
Trinity College, box 6000
Hartford, Connecticut 06106
(203) 247-2735
contact: Ed Mierzwinski,
    director

Florida PIRG (FPIRG)
Florida State University
P.O. Box U-6367
Tallahassee, Florida 32313
(904) 644-2826
contact: Neil Friedman,
    director

**Idaho PIRG (organizing
    committee)**
c/o The University News
Boise State University
1910 University Dr.
Boise, Idaho 83725
(208) 385-1464
contact: Brad Martin, Janice
    Pavlick

Illinois PIRG (IPIRG)
Southern Illinois University
Box 168, SIUE
Edwardsville, Illinois 62026
(618) 692-3382
contact: Tim Earley, director

Indiana PIRG (InPIRG)
406 N. Fess St.
Bloomington, Indiana 47405
(812) 335-7575
contact: Larry Nelson,
    director

Iowa PIRG
Iowa State University
Memorial Union, room 36
Ames, Iowa 50011
(515) 294-8094
contact: Steve deProff

Maine PIRG (USMPIRG)
92 Bedford St.
Portland, Maine 04103
(207) 780-4044
contact: Donna Jones,
    director

Maryland PIRG (MaryPIRG)
3110 Main Dining Hall
University of Maryland
College Park, Maryland 20742
(301) 454-5601
contact: Theresa Mulliken,
    director

Massachusetts PIRG (MassPIRG)
37 Temple Pl.
Boston, Massachusetts 02111
(617) 423-1796
contact: Doug Phelps,
    director

PIRG in Michigan (PIRGIM)
590 Hollister Bldg.
206 W. Allegan St.
Lansing, Michigan 48933
(517) 487-6001
contact: J. D. Snyder,
    director

Minnesota PIRG (MPIRG)
2412 University Ave., S.E.
Minneapolis, Minnesota 55414
(612) 376-7554
contact: Jim Miller, director

Missouri PIRG (MoPIRG)
Box 8276
St. Louis, Missouri 63156
(314) 534-7474
contact: Tom Ryan,
    director

Montana PIRG (MontPIRG)
729 Keith
Missoula, Montana 59801
(406) 721-6040

contact: C.B. Pearson,
    director

New Jersey PIRG (NJPIRG)
204 W. State St.
Trenton, NJ 08608
(609) 393-7474
contact: Ed Lloyd, director

New Mexico PIRG (NMPIRG)
University of New Mexico
Box 66, SUB
Albuquerque, NM 87131
(505) 277-2757
contact: Richard Hall,
    director

New York PIRG (NYPIRG)
9 Murray St.
New York, New York 10007
(212) 349-6460
contact: Marilyn Ondrasik,
    director

North Carolina PIRG (NCPIRG)
704½ Ninth St.
P.O. Box 2901
Durham, North Carolina 27705
(919) 286-2275
contact: Ruffin Slater, director

Ohio PIRG (OPIRG)
65 So. Fourth St.
Columbus, Ohio 43215
(614) 461-0136
contact: Nancy Bartter, Juli
    Neander, co-directors

Oregon Student PIRG (OSPIRG)
Box 751, Portland State University
Portland, Oregon 97207
(503) 229-4500
contact: Jon Stubenvoll

Rhode Island PIRG (RIPIRG)
University of Rhode Island

Room 145, Memorial Union
Kingston, Rhode Island 02881
(401) 792-2585
contact: Ken Ward, director

Texas PIRG (TexPIRG)
Rice University, 6100 South
Lane
Houston, Texas 77005
(713) 527-4099

**Utah PIRG (organizing
committee)**
University of Utah Union 149
Salt Lake City, Utah 84112
(801) 581-3128
contact: Jeff Worsham

Virginia PIRG (VaPIRG)
College of William and Mary
Campus Center
Williamsburg, Virginia 23185
(804) 253-4602

contact: Steve Salter,
organizer

Washington PIRG (WashPIRG)
University of Washington
Student Union Bldg. FK-30
Seattle, Washington 98195
(206) 543-0434
contact: Danny Kadden,
organizer

**Wisconsin PIRG (organizing
committee)**
c/o Mitch Batuzich
309 N. Mills
Madison, WI 53715
(608) 255-5296

**Wyoming PIRG (organizing
committee)**
c/o David Kane
572 North 6th
Laramie, Wyoming 82070

DIRECTORY OF PUBLIC INTEREST GROUPS AND PUBLICATIONS

The Public Citizen network in Washington, founded by Ralph Nader, is very active on the federal level in some of the areas PIRG work in on the state level. Here are descriptions of the Public Citizen groups, with their addresses. Many of their publications are listed below.

ORGANIZATIONS

The **Health Research Group** works to inform consumers about issues that affect their health and to challenge health-related regulatory agencies to do their job of protecting the public. The group petitions federal agencies, prepares congressional testimony, and monitors health and safety legislation. It also publicizes important findings and distributes consumer information and action materials. 2000 P St., N. W., room 708, Washington, D.C. 20036, (202) 872-0320.

The **Critical Mass Energy Project** works for an end to nuclear power development in favor of safe energy alternatives. Recent projects and issues have included emergency planning, reactor safety, and transition from nuclear to solar energy. 215 Pennsylvania Ave., S. E., Washington, D.C. 20003, (202) 546-4790.

Congress Watch is the legislative advocacy arm of Public Citizen, whose attorneys, organizers, and other staff represent the citizen/consumer before the U.S. Congress. Recent projects have included working to preserve solar and conservation funds in the federal budget; eliminating government subsidies for special interests; maintaining safety and fuel efficiency standards in automobiles, closing unfair tax loopholes; reforming regulatory and health requirements; and others. 215 Pennsylvania Ave., S. E., Washington, D.C. 20003, (202) 546-4996.

The **Litigation Group** conducts litigation concerning broad government policies and private actions with widespread public impact. Recent issues have included energy, labor, health, corporate accountability and freedom of information. 2000 P St., N.W. room 700, Washington, D.C. 20036, (202) 785-3704.

The **Tax Reform Research Group** works for progressive tax reform at the national, state, and local level. The group's

activities include working in Congress, monitoring the Internal Revenue Service, and assisting local groups. 215 Pennsylvania Ave., S. E., Washington, D.C. 20003, (202) 544-1710.

Other colleague groups include: The **Center for Auto Safety**, which works to reduce deaths from defective automobiles and badly constructed highways, and advises consumers and attorneys on warranties and other legal rights. 1346 Connecticut Ave., N.W., room 1223, Washington, D.C. 20036, (202) 659-1126; the **Center for Science in the Public Interest**, which provides the public with information about the effects of science and technology on society, with a major focus on food and health. 1755 S. St., N.W., Washington, D.C. 20009, (202) 332-9110; the **Clean Water Action Project**, which works at eliminating water pollution, safeguarding drinking water, and protecting water resources and wetlands. 1341 G St., N.W., room 200, Washington, D.C. 20005, (202) 462-2520; the **National Insurance Consumer Organization**, which educates insurance consumers and works to reform insurance institutions. 344 Commerce St., Alexandria, VA 22314, (703) 549-8050; and the **Pension Rights Center**, which protects and promotes the rights of people who look to pension plans as a secure retirement income. 1346 Connecticut Ave., N.W., Washington, D.C. 20036, (202) 296-3778.

PUBLICATIONS

The Congress Watcher is a 16 page bi-monthly newspaper published by *Congress Watch,* which covers a variety of consumer, energy, and environmental issues. **The Congress Watcher** includes updates on important federal legislation, reports on Congress Watch locals in several states, occasional profiles of members of Congress, and information on campaign finance and lobbying. A year's subscription is $5.00, available from *Congress Watch.*

Congress Watch also produces annual Congressional Voting Records, which chart the votes of each Representative and Senator on dozens of consumer, environmental, and energy bills. The voting records usually include some information on campaign contributions as well. The 1982 voting record report is available from Congress Watch for $5.00.

The **Critical Mass Energy Journal,** the monthly newspaper of the *Critical Mass Energy Proj-*

ect, gives extensive coverage of nuclear and alternative energy issues, including articles on energy regulation, federal legislation, nuclear and alternative energy issues, including articles on energy regulation, federal legislation, nuclear energy safety, and local safe energy movements. The Journal is available for $10.00 for one year. The **Journal** has a regular, detailed resources section and offers reprints of key **Journal** articles. *Critical Mass* has a special offer of cash rebates for local safe energy groups which sell **Journal** subscriptions; write for details.

People & Taxes is the monthly newspaper of the *Tax Reform Research Group*, which covers federal tax legislation, IRS practices, and state and local tax policy. **P&T** also publishes annual special editions on taxpayer assistance in March and April, and regularly publicizes congressional voting records on tax and finance issues. A year's subscription is $10.00.

Tax Politics is an excellent, readable book on tax reform. Written by *Tax Reform Research Group* staff in 1976, it covers federal tax policy, information on how Congress passes tax bills, IRS procedures, and state and local tax issues. The Tax Group offers a discount on **Tax Politics** with a subscription to **People & Taxes;** write for details.

Public Citizen is the quarterly magazine for *Public Citizen* doners. It covers the activities and accomplishments of all the *Public Citizen* groups, and features major articles on national issues. Free with $15.00 annual contribution to *Public Citizen,* P.O. Box 19404, Washington, D.C. 20036.

Changing More Than the Channel: A Citizens Guide to Forming a Media Access Group is a simple but comprehensive guide for citizens and public interest groups seeking to increase broadcaster responsiveness to the community. Available for $6.00 from the *National Citizens Committee on Broadcasting,* P.O. Box 12038, Washington, D.C. 20005.

The **Citizens Guide to Periodicals of Public Interest Groups** lists scores of newsletters, newspapers, and magazines of public interest organizations. The Guide is available for $5.00 from the Commission for the Advancement of Public Interest Organizations, 1875 Connecticut Ave., N.W., Washington, D.C. 20009.

Good Works is a unique, thorough guide to full-time jobs and student internships in the public interest. Produced by the *Center for Study of Responsive Law,* **Good Works** provides information on hundreds of social change organizations, the types of jobs available in them, and how to apply. It also features profiles of some people working for these organizations, which discuss more about what motivates them, and what exactly their work entails. The volume is available for $25.00 from the Center, P.O. Box 19367, Washington, D.C. 20036. If your library doesn't have this book, urge them to order it.

Other Center publication include **For the People** ($5.95), with step-by-step approaches to community action; **Hucksters in the Classroom** ($10.00), which looks at the wide-spread use in classrooms of industry-produced materials promoting corporate goals; **American Universities: Who Pays for Them, Who Runs Them and Who Profits** ($2.50); **Energy Conservation: A Campus Guidebook** ($3.00); and **A Student's Guide to Improving Food Services** ($5.00). The Center also has a publication list, "Writing for You," which is free with a stamped, self-addressed envelope.

Reagan's Ruling Class, Profiles of the President's Top 100 Officials. The book gives a candid look into the power structure of the Reagan Administration, the backgrounds of the chief officials, and the policies they espouse. It is available for $24.50 from the *Learning Research Project,* P.O. Box 19312, Washington, D.C. 20036.

Who Runs Congress? offers a good look at how Congress works, who has the power, and why. Written by Mark Green, former *Congress Watch* director, **Who Runs Congress** has detailed chapters on the influence of lobbying and campaign finance, as well as a "primer for citizen action." Published by Bantam Books, $2.95.

Winning Back America, also by Mark Green, is a collection of progressive approaches to a variety of issues, from unemployment to the environment. Published by Bantam books, $3.95.

Index